Praise for

PROFIT FROM EXPERIENCE

"This is far more than a   book—it is a blueprint for individual (

Rich

Senio
Devel
Author of *Inside Teams*

"Fills a void in today's quick-fix environment. Reengineering the self is at the core of organizational change. An excellent handbook to support leadership development programs."

Michael R. Plummer
Manager, Organization Development
AT&T Universal Card Services

"A commitment to continuous learning is the differentiator between a champion and a contender. This book challenges each of us to make the commitment to become a champion!"

Jerre Stead
CEO
Legent Corp

"Experience can be the best teacher if we reflect on it. You don't read this book—you use it! Then you prosper."

Jim Kouzes
Coauthor of *The Leadership Challenge* and *Credibility*
President
Tom Peters Group/Learning Systems

"**A** provocative and surprisingly deep approach that could turn around your life—or your organization."

John Scherer
Founder
Center for Work and the Human Spirit

"**M**akes personal change stick! The quotes throughout are very thought provoking—wonderful."

Katie Birthler
Vice President, Human Resources
North American Bakery
Multifoods Corporation

"**I**f you don't have time to even read a book, then make time to read this one. It could give you time to read more, plan more, and become more of yourself."

Geoffrey M. Bellman
Author of *Getting Things Done When You're Not in Charge*

"**A** useful, practical approach for assessing my current reality."

Carol Spicer
Director: Leadership Effectiveness
U.S. West Communication

"**O**n the cutting edge of how each of us is repsonsible for the world we experience, this is a book that touches the spirit – yet provides practical, doable exercises to incorporate the spiritual into daily work."

Gerald C. Swanson
Engineering Improvement Manager,
Boeing Commercial Aircraft

Dr. Michael J. O'Brien

PROFIT FROM EXPERIENCE

A Guide to Knowing Yourself and Influencing Others

Michael J. O'Brien
with Larry Shook

SOMBRERO PRESS
SPOKANE, WASHINGTON

an imprint of
THE PRINTED WORD INC.
P.O. Box 31166 • Spokane, WA 99223
www.SombreroPress.com

Library of Congress Cataloging-in-Publication Data
O'Brien, Michael J. (Michael James), 1953-
    Profit from experience : a guide to knowing yourself and influencing others / Michael J. O'Brien with Larry Shook.
        p. cm.
    Includes bibliographical references and index.
    ISBN-13: 978-1-934738-26-9 (alk. paper)
    ISBN-10: 1-934738-26-3
    1. Self-actualization (Psychology) 2. Change (Psychology) I. Shook, Larry. II. Title.
    BF637.S4O27 2009
    158.1–dc22

                        2009041640

ISBN-13: 978-1-934738-26-9
ISBN-10: 1-934738-26-3

PRINTING HISTORY
Bard & Stephen edition / May 1995
Berkley trade paperback edition / July 1998
O'Brien Group edition / October 2003
Sombrero Press edition / November 2009

10 9 8 7 6 5 4 3 2 1

Printed in the United States of America

The corporate mission of The Printed Word Inc.: *inform, uplift & empower*

To Beverly,
with love,
for your continual support,
constant encouragement,
and frequent inspiration.

Contents

The Days

The Exercises

About the Authors

MICHAEL J. O'BRIEN is founder and president of The O'Brien Group, an executive coaching and leadership development consulting firm. Michael holds a doctorate in corporate training and human resource development and a master's in education. His areas of concentration are cognitive psychology and organizational psychology. For over twenty years he has consulted with corporate clients, including AT&T, General Electric, Xerox, Schering-Plough, McDonnell Douglas, Prudential, Bayer Corporation, NYNEX, and Bell Atlantic. He is author of the *Learning Organization Practices Profile* (Jossey-Bass) and numerous articles on organizational learning and leadership development. Michael lives with his wife, Beverly, and children, Douglas and Mary, in Cincinnati, Ohio.

LARRY SHOOK is a writer, editor, and publisher who has contributed to such national publications as the *Washington Post,* the *New York Times,* and *People* magazine. He is author of *The Quality Detective's Bedside Companion* and coauthor of *Work and the Human Spirit.* Formerly editor of *San Diego Magazine, Spokane Magazine,* and *Washington Magazine,* he is now president of The Printed Word, a communications company. Larry lives with his wife, Judy, and children, Ben and Katie, in Spokane, Washington.

Acknowledgments

THIS BOOK WAS TRULY A LABOR OF LOVE and intention on the part of many people. I would like to acknowledge and thank all the clients, friends, family, and associates who reviewed the many iterations of the manuscript and gave me moral support.

I would especially like to thank those associates who, over the last two years, have contributed in special ways to my writing: John Scherer, for blazing a trail and giving me lots of advice; Judy Laddon, for continuous feedback and technical support; and Ron Kirsch, Diane Russ, and Doug Cohen, for the many discussions that helped clarify concepts and principles.

Special thanks also to Robyn Renner and Arlene Beauchemin, two very dear clients who have provided me many opportunities to both teach and learn.

Finally, thanks to Larry Shook, my writing partner, for helping me express what was on my mind and in my heart.

Getting Ready to Grow

*"The future of work
consists of __learning__ a living."*

— MARSHALL MCLUHAN

PROFIT FROM EXPERIENCE is based on two assumptions. First, we live in an age when dramatic personal change is required of all of us. Second, systematically learning from experience is the best means at our disposal for changing in the ways we need to.

The problem is (and we have to say this, because the evidence is overwhelming) that learning from experience is not automatic, either for individuals or for society. It is all too natural for people and organizations, or even civilizations, to make the same mistakes over and over again.

What happens consistently is that people don't notice when change is required. To actually learn something new from experience requires an intentional and disciplined effort.

Why You Should Read This Book

PROFIT FROM EXPERIENCE is offered as a handbook, and a field book, of personal change. Because the world around us is changing so profoundly, the least adaptive among us are being ruthlessly weeded out—professionally, emotionally, and even physically. To be able to learn, to consciously change and improve your patterns of behavior, will dramatically increase your personal effectiveness.

Many of us today are faced with the need to learn some of the most important lessons of our lives. Professionally, the learning mandate ranges from such matters as how to lead a team, how to influence people you're not the boss of, how to take on one more project when you're booked solid. Personally, most of us are dealing with such issues as the need to find more constructive resolutions to conflict in intimate relationships, raising children in an age when the stakes of peer pressure are higher than ever, finding calm in the midst of stress.

The methods in this book—which require small, daily effort—can help you inventory the areas of your life where change is most needed. The methods will then help you start producing the life results you're looking for.

Creative Tension

IF YOU CHOOSE TO ACCEPT THE MISSION of profiting from your experience, the profit you realize will come from the creative tension that steady discipline brings about.

To understand the kind of tension I'm talking about, hold a rubber band between your two hands, and stretch it tight by moving your right hand away. Move as far with your right hand as you can without breaking the rubber band. Feel the tension.

Before going any further, notice that you have already made at least one choice. You have decided to go get a rubber band, or not, and you have decided how tightly to stretch it.

The rubber band is a metaphor for life.

Think of your left hand as the status quo, your circumstances as they presently exist. Think of your right hand as the direction in which you would like to move.

Now, relax the tension on the rubber band by moving *only one hand.*

Once again, you made a decision. Your hands didn't decide. The rubber band didn't decide. Did you go to the left or the right?

The natural choice, by the way, is to let the right hand move back to the left, the status quo. Nobody likes to change. Why fix what ain't broke? If that was your choice, you now have to think about something else. Namely, was the decision not to change a good one, or should you reconsider? This choice, too, is yours alone. You can't avoid making choices.

By the way, even though this may strike you as a simple idea, if you didn't actually pick up a rubber band and perform the demonstration, you still can't grasp the point. A major premise of this book is that intellectual understanding alone is inadequate.

Simply having this kind of internal conversation can change your life. It reflects heightened consciousness and persistent self-reflection. We control our destinies in direct proportion to our self-awareness. Two thousand years ago a Chinese sage, Lao Tsu, put it this way: "Those who know

We control our destinies in direct proportion to our self-awareness.

much about others may be smart, but those who understand themselves are even wiser. Those who control many may be powerful, but those who have mastered themselves are more powerful still."

There is nothing exotic about the techniques you are about to learn. Like most ideas, these are mostly borrowed. They are simply arranged here in a way that many of my clients and I have found helpful. They really will produce creative tension in your life, and the tension will at least cause you to choose how, or whether, you want to learn something new.

Looking Within

ACCORDING TO HINDU LEGEND, there was a time on Earth when people possessed the wisdom of the gods. But the veil of physical life kept human beings from fully appreciating this gift. Brahma concluded that it was wrong to leave such precious treasure lying at the feet of sleepwalkers. So he decided to hide it where only the most persistent would ever discover it.

"Let's bury it deep in the earth," one god suggested.

"No," replied Brahma. "People will dig down in the earth and find it."

"Then let's put it in the deepest ocean," said another.

Brahma rejected that idea, too. "People will learn to dive and will find it someday," he said.

A third god asked, "Why don't we hide it on the highest mountain?"

Brahma answered, "No, people can climb the highest mountain. I have a better place. Let's hide it deep inside the people themselves; they'll never think to look there."

Committing to Action

THIS BOOK GREW OUT OF YEARS OF WORK I have done with large organizations. For the most part, these organizations are run by people with more than enough education, intelligence, and expertise. But time and again I see executives and managers do something irrational and inexplicable. On the one hand, they grasp new concepts of learning, growing, improving. Then they turn around and go back to their old ways, making decisions and interacting with others just as they always have, as if they've learned nothing and don't need to change at all.

Concepts of profound personal and organizational renewal are easy to understand. Acting on them takes discipline, plus a personal commitment to learn, and go on learning, what our changing environment has to teach. The material in this book is a balance of concept and action—daily action, constant action. Without the action, the concepts are interesting but not much else.

Most of us don't learn useful things from our experiences, at least not consistently. Our learning is often by accident, and it doesn't come easily. We often learn dysfunctional behaviors—hating or blaming other people, pouting, being depressed. What we want, of course, is to learn how to think and behave in ways that accomplish our purposes with grace and flexibility.

What follows are some ideas and exercises that will start you on an expedition to uncover the treasure Brahma hid within you. Happy hunting.

"A successful career will no longer be about promotion. It will be about mastery."

—MICHAEL HAMMER

Personal Change:
Why Is It So Hard?

"Old habits are strong and jealous."

—Dorothea Brande

Today we know there's physiological evidence for Pogo's famous observation—"We have met the enemy and he is us." The enemy, apparently, is between our ears.

The good news is the brain's phenomenal power. It's estimated that a single human brain has the switching capacity of the entire U.S. telephone network. It can hold up to 100 trillion bits of information, dwarfing the capacity of any computer in the land.

The bad news is that the brain can act as a prison unless we learn how to control it. The brain can, and often does, lock us into automatic perceptions and behaviors that are inaccurate, ineffective, or downright destructive.

How the human brain works is worth noting if we want to change.

At birth it is a uniquely incomplete work of art. No other newborn creature experiences such brain expansion—doubling in the first six months, then again by age four.

Simultaneously, the body's hundred billion nerve cells form a river of information that saturates every organ, every muscle, with perception, with knowledge, with memory. When something happens—an event, a thought—neurotransmitters flash across synapses in twinkle-sized units of time. In a nanosecond the experience of life has impressed itself into our blood, our bones, our brains. Before we know it, our lives are being composed.

Our life experiences shape our view of the world.

So here is a basic reality: *our life experiences shape our view of the world.* Not only psychologically, but physically. Throughout childhood, the human brain is a frenzied construction site, where neural structures are assembled in response to events and thoughts, and countless circuits in the brain are rushed to completion. In the course of this construction, some connections are bolstered into massive conduits of habit. Others are systematically diminished and sometimes even dismantled.

Hard-Wiring of the Adolescent

THE INTENSIVE BRAIN DEVELOPMENT of early childhood is followed by an amazing event. During a single three-week period of adolescence, power to the construction site of the brain is drastically cut back. The brain's metabolism falls to half its previous rate.

This occurs in the life of every individual, and it so profoundly impacts the way we lead our lives, it might actually be the single most important event in each of our lives. Why? Because it locks us into a way of being that will govern our lives more force-fully, and more ruthlessly, than any tyrant.

Of course, we can all change and adapt well into old age. It's just that until this point in time, learning comes much more easily. The child's natural philosophy is "I don't know how the world works. . . . Tell me, show me, feed me."

After that three-week passage into neural maturity—a passage that coincides with the ability to reproduce—the young adult's philosophy becomes "Now I know about the world. . . . I'll tell you."

Dr. Robert B. Livingston, who has been a professor at Stanford, Yale, Harvard, and UCLA, and who is considered one of America's foremost brain researchers, points out that at this unconscious and momentous turning point in adolescence, our experience of the world becomes "biologically wired into the brain." In the journal *Timeline* he described it this way:

> You're no longer so smart, so quick, so good at remembering or building new circuits. Already unique to begin with, genetically, you have made a nervous system that is astonishingly unique, and your programmed world view becomes quite frozen. It is well defended and sacred, and nobody can change it. It's stuck there, culture bound, bound by your past experience, bound in accordance with your purpose at the particular moment. And it is guarded automatically and involuntarily because your life depends on it. If you ride a bicycle, you don't have time to have a

parliament in the head when an immediate response is required; you have to act now.

So there you have it. At age thirteen (or twelve or fourteen, whenever your turning point occurred), your brain said, "Fantastic! Good enough! We're finished! Lower the scaffolds. It's time to go home."

And one would hope that your parents, and your siblings, your teachers, aunts and uncles, grandparents, and all your friends, your society, even your enemies or critics, were brilliantly synchronized and lovingly coordinated to program and enrich your brain so that it would serve your highest goals, all your life long.

But if your brain's software has some glitches, if your universe doesn't reflect the harmony, beauty, love, and fulfillment that you deserve, then you might want to learn the "art of consciousness," the ability to become master of the self instead of its slave.

Mastering the Self

To TRULY KNOW ONESELF is to explore the huge range of responses and creative acts that we can bring to life instead of the narrow repertoire of past habits we call the personality. At the heart of this lesson is a priceless insight: though you *have* a mind, you are *not* your mind. You are the one who administers the mind, Chief Executive Officer of the self. Who you are is the one who can change your mind, change your programming.

We aren't taught this, the art of consciousness, in school. This is a curious oversight in a society that celebrates liberty, for without the ability to control the mind no one can ever be free, no matter the military might of one's country. The art of consciousness is a skill that has been singularly lacking throughout history, and this may help explain why history repeats itself. It certainly explains why most of us spend our lives making many of the same mistakes over and over. There is no question that a critical mass of people practicing the art of consciousness would change the course of history. There is no question that those who become conscious, who come into their right minds, do change their own lives in proportion to their self-awareness.

Though you have a mind, you are not your mind.

The ability of people to become truly self-aware, to learn continuously from experience, and to constantly choose from an infinite range of viewpoints and actions those that promise the best results, instead of those that are most familiar and require the least change, is the breakthrough upon which the future of humanity might well depend. Closer to home, it might mean the future of a job, a career, an important relationship, prosperity, health, or an inner sense of gratification and serenity.

Changing Your World View

SO THIS EXOTIC MISSION, to change the hard-wiring of your brain, is before you. If you choose to accept it, you need to know the bad news: this kind of change is very hard. But the good news is that it's easier than overcoming a physical dependency, such as alcoholism or smoking—and people manage to shake such addictions all the time.

Besides, learning is inherently rewarding. Research shows that the brain responds to learning much as muscle responds to exercise—that is, strong, new, life-supporting tissue is created. In the brain, the new tissue is actually the synaptic connecting matter between brain cells. Evidence suggests that a healthy network of these neural branches—they're called dendrites and they resemble a meandering river system—may, among other things, delay the onset of Alzheimer's disease and aid in recovery from strokes.

The brain responds to learning much as muscle responds to exercise.

Dr. Livingston offers a straightforward prescription for improving the brain's hard-wiring:

If you want to shift somebody's world view, you have to get them to spend a lot of time thinking about alternative world views, spend a lot of time encouraging them, seducing them, exercising in that new equilibrium state so that they become familiar with it and know whether or not they like it better than the old one. Suddenly, they realize that they've been captured; it's like a transformation, a religious conversion, like falling in love. And when that happens, it has a long duration. It may last forever. You have a different attitude toward everybody on the globe. You are a different person, you have different commitments, you have different judgments in relation to everything—economics, society, language—

you can't put your finger on any part of your life that isn't affected by that conversion. And it makes it easy and automatic to operate once you're in that new equilibrium. You don't have to resort to apologies or going back to see what it would look like from the old vantage point. You just proceed head on.

A woman I know had an experience that illustrates Dr. Livingston's point. She was working as a registered nurse in the child psychiatric unit of a hospital. As it turned out, many of her colleagues, men and women, were gay. My friend had been raised in a fundamentalist Christian home and had deep prejudices regarding homosexuals.

On top of the tremendous stress of the job, the unit was small, which meant that staff worked shoulder to shoulder, often literally wrestling together with their young charges. For many months my friend couldn't shake the considerable discomfort she felt at working with homosexuals.

And then something happened. It slowly dawned on her that she respected her colleagues. Not only were they skillful, they were unusually loving and compassionate people. They epitomized the ideals of nursing. And yet, they had unaccountably chosen a lifestyle that my friend believed to be wrong.

One day she asked a male colleague a personal question: had he ever tried being with a woman? In deepest sincerity, she suggested that if he would just date a few women he might find that he was, well, normal after all. The man could see that my friend cared for him and that she meant well. With equal sincerity, he asked her how she knew that she was heterosexual. Had she ever just tried being with a woman?

For some reason, that one question was like an earthquake. In an instant, as surely as she knew that her own sexual orientation was not an issue in her life, she realized that the sexuality of others no longer was either. In the blink of an eye, what had been a painful barrier between her and her co-workers vanished.

An added bonus of this shift: my friend reports she has never again felt separated from others simply because they are different from her.

The Currents of Change

CHANGE IS A RIVER WITH MANY HEADWATERS, and those who study the watershed are filing interesting reports these days. Political observers, for instance, tell us that because of rapid social change, the maps of our school days are really antiques and should be replaced by three-dimensional cartography. Borders are giving way to moving centers of power, a trait of the Middle Ages. And, as environmental experts like Barbara Tuchman Matthews warn, the world's policy makers haven't even begun to realize the extent to which modern societies "depend on the underpinning of natural systems"—natural systems that are being worn away by a variety of pressures.

Meanwhile, one of the most common of all elements, information, is transforming our economic foundations. Information has become more valuable than precious metals, water, or oil. More than any other resource, it may soon separate have from have-not nations.

Who knows where these trends will lead? At least in human terms, ours is an old planet. Big things happen from time to time. If all the world's a stage and all its people players . . . well, then, you might say that every so often the Great Playwright rearranges the set and edits the script. The climate changes, plagues sweep the countryside, landforms get moved around like props, plants and animals come and go.

How will the human imagination be used, how will the *will* be focused, what values and new skills will sculpt our lives? None of us can control the world, of course, but each of us—alone—controls his or her response to it. Choice is a basic force in human affairs, a powerful force, and our choices form headwaters of their own. Of course the world shapes us; but we shape our world, too.

Of course the world shapes us; but we shape our world, too.

In the world of business, not so very long ago, people who worked on "improving themselves," people who read "self-help" books and occasionally slipped away to weekend seminars about how to find themselves, these people were seen as . . . well, eccentric . . . soft, somehow. If they ran into each other at a workshop, they would acknowledge one another furtively, like illegal aliens. They knew that back in the real world of the mainstream their willingness to explore the examined life made them irresistible targets of satire. Even in today's enlightened times, such fear is not without basis.

27

In a cartoon featured in the *Harvard Business Review*, for example, an executive fresh from a training retreat says to colleagues around a conference table: "Before we begin the meeting, I'd like everyone to relax by crowing like a rooster."

By and large, however, the business press doesn't make fun of personal change as much as it used to. This might be because the old, reliable formulas for success and profitability are being swept away by tidal waves of collapsed markets, unwieldy bureaucracies, and rampant technological changes.

Just stop for a moment and consider your own career path. Are you doing what you prepared to do in college? Has your career path been what you thought it would be? How many different organizations have you worked for in the last 10 to 20 years? If you *are* in the same career you trained for, how have technology, market forces and competition changed the way you do your work?

No wonder *Fortune* magazine is urging its readers to wake up and smell the coffee. In an article called "A Manager's Career in the New Economy," it set forth an assortment of sobering possibilities like these:

- Regular jobs may evaporate, replaced by hand-picked task forces that come together for specific projects, then disband when the projects are over.

- The American economy will be transformed into "one-person organizations" as information technology, especially the computer network, allows more and more work to be outsourced. (One MIT professor says that a global network of one-person companies could actually design, manufacture, and market a new car right now.)

- "Hyperspecialists" are about to inherit an electronically unified global marketplace.
- Managers as a higher-paid class of workers are about to go the way of the passenger pigeon because their services will no longer add enough value to justify their higher pay.

Fortune didn't go too far out on a limb when it peered into its crystal ball and predicted that "millions, perhaps the majority of the population, will be troubled by the change." But the most troubling thing won't be just that the work is new, but that only a new kind of worker will be able to do it.

Fortune came right out and said it: "Know thyself." Since when has that ever been a job requirement? Welcome to the new world. *Fortune* put it this way:

"The key to success, perhaps even to survival, in the new world is, pardon the already too familiar expression, lifelong learning. For managers and executives, the most painful learning—like knowing thyself—may prove the most valuable."

For their book *Credibility: How Leaders Gain and Lose It, Why People Demand It*, James Kouzes and Barry Posner asked fifteen thousand working people to assess the leaders in their lives. The verdict they were handed was that the foundation of the relationship between leaders and employees has crumbled. Yet workers are searching for leaders "who are honest, forward-looking, inspiring, and competent." These are the qualities that add up to credibility, the backbone of leadership, say Kouzes and Posner. They propose a personal regimen whereby leaders can cultivate credibility. Their first recommendation: continuously explore the inner self.

Accepting the Mission

THIS BOOK IS DESIGNED TO ASSIST PEOPLE in this exploration. Because real learning has to leap the awkward chasm from thought to action, I have incorporated a few exercises that I humbly suggest you do.

There's nothing esoteric about these exercises. If any of them don't seem to work for you, fine. Move along to the next one without guilt. There are no universal formulas. The sequence in which you do the exercises isn't especially critical. More than anything else, they will simply provide you with a stimulus for new ways of thinking, integrated into some form of action.

In more than fifteen years of coaching executives in the art of consciousness, I have seen repeatedly that hard-wired habit usually cannot be changed with new understanding alone. The learning and changing most people want comes about through small, daily *practice* of new behaviors and thoughts.

There is considerable evidence supporting the

premise that it takes most people twenty-one days to change habits—that is, to experience and integrate new behaviors. That's why this book is designed to be used over that period of time. But don't be hung up on that number. The point is, this technology is designed to produce real change that is otherwise difficult. It is not a quick fix. In the overall scheme of your life, a half hour a day for twenty-one days is not a big deal, but it *is* an investment. Take three or four weeks to learn the discipline; take the rest of your life to practice. If it takes you two or three months to get through these exercises, that's fine. Skip around if you like. Respect your own rhythm of learning.

Learning and changing come about through small, daily practice of new behaviors and thoughts.

First step: get yourself a notebook to be used as a journal. Or, use the journal pages at the end of this book. In the journal you will do the written exercises, make notes about your progress, and record your thoughts.

In case you're wondering why you should go to the trouble of actually writing down your responses to the exercises, I'd like to share an answer given to me by one of the people kind enough to review this book in an earlier, manuscript form. "Journaling," he said, "takes away the wiggle room you can leave yourself as you ponder these questions."

Wonderful image. There is no surer way *not* to profit from experience than by wiggling away from the sometimes uncomfortable lessons that tough issues bring.

If you don't want to do any exercises, but just want to read, you may find the book interesting, but in all likelihood it won't prove to be especially useful. In order to use *Profit from Experience* for actual growth and development, you'll need to incorporate the new patterns into your life in a disciplined way.

One last thing: be kind to yourself in doing the exercises. If you feel resistant to some of them—or even intimidated—just know that can be a signal an exercise holds special value for you. But don't bludgeon yourself into doing it. Proceed with patience and kindness. Teachers of meditation like to use the phrase "training the puppy" as a way of describing the gentleness required to gain maximum benefit from the practice. That is the proper spirit with which to incorporate the *Profit from Experience* exercises into your life. The idea is to be gentle but clear.

> *"In a time of drastic change it is the learners who inherit the future. The learned usually find themselves equipped to live in a world that no longer exists."*
>
> —ERIC HOFFER

day 1

Personal Mastery

"Real education consists in drawing the best out of yourself."

—MOHANDAS GANDHI

PERSONAL MASTERY—the practice of intentional change—is a little like the search for El Dorado, the lost city of gold. Or the Fountain of Youth. That's what the notion of personal change—*real* change—seems like to a lot of us: a fairy tale.

And yet, the benefits of personal mastery—profound personal satisfaction and rewarding productivity, among others—are ends that most of us strive for in one way or another.

Still, skepticism about our ability to change is understandable. I've mentioned a few reasons why. If inside each of us is a petulant young adult who rebels against being taught anything new, who thinks he or she already knows everything, it's no wonder there are a few skeptics and pessimists among us.

Change Is Possible

THE TRUTH IS, you really can change yourself. It is just very hard. And you can't do it with New Year's resolutions, with wishing and hoping alone. And you certainly can't do it by simply understanding the theory of personal change, which isn't all that hard to grasp.

The ideas and daily actions I'm presenting here don't embody the *only* way to change. Fortunately, in our culture we are experiencing a wealth of shared wisdom and insights for personal improvement. But these daily recommendations definitely are *a* way to master and improve your life and, by extension, your organization or business.

If you take a few minutes every day, both reviewing the ideas and taking the actions I recommend, you will definitely experience dramatic results. First of all, you will figure out the ground rules for having a satisfied mind. Then you will notice your relationships with others improving, conversations and meetings will be more satisfying, your priorities and values will be more a part of your life. And long after you've finished this book, you can continue to reap rewards. You will know how to learn from experience, how to learn from the events life presents to you and the experiences you yourself create. You will have learned the gentle discipline of change through daily practice.

Thinking about Changing

WOVEN INTO the *Profit from Experience* methodology are four overlapping practices:

- Raising consciousness
- Imagining
- Framing and reframing
- Integrating new perspectives

They aren't always named as such in the exercises, but they are the mental and physical mechanisms at work.

Raising your consciousness means not just thinking, but thinking *about* thinking, noticing—and managing—the workings of your mind so your mind won't run away with your life like a startled horse. Simple and immediate ways of raising your consciousness are discussed later in more detail. Practice them; chances are you'll notice an immediate improvement in your quality of life.

Raising consciousness means not just thinking, but thinking about thinking.

When you *imagine,* you create a mental picture—the most vivid image you can—of an outcome you desire. Does it work? You bet it does, and you do it all the time. If you're typical, however, most of the imagining you do goes by another name: worry. This most common form of imagining leads not to something you want but to something you don't, and it works depressingly well.

Framing and reframing form the very foundation of the human experience. They are the essence of personal freedom. They are about interpreting the world, making meaning, assigning significance to the events of life. When two thousand years ago the Greek Stoic Epictetus noted that it is not the events of life that matter but our opinion of them, he was talking about framing and reframing. You don't have to think of anything in any particular way. You can think of green as white if you wish. But some ways of thinking about things are more helpful than others. Learning to frame and reframe means learning to see things in the most helpful light, that's all.

When Robert Livingston refers to changing one's world view, he is describing what happens when you integrate new perspectives. What we see depends on where we stand. And where we stand— that is, the view of the world our senses present to us—is profoundly influenced by the biases of our family of origin and the hand fate dealt us. Thank heaven we're not stuck with just one world view. We can get a new one any time merely by learning to integrate the perspectives of others. In this sense, the points of view of other people rank among life's most priceless gifts.

Changing the World

IT IS ARBITRARY TO THINK of these four practices for creating personal change as separate. In reality, they flow into and out of one another. Engage in any one of them and you inevitably elevate your consciousness. Integrate the perspective of another and you reframe your own viewpoint.

If you consistently weave the practices together, day after day, they will become second nature. When that happens, your *first nature* will shift. That is, the pattern of your thoughts will change— it may be that the very cells of your body will be rearranged in response to the electrochemical impulses of changed thoughts—and your world view will be different.

What you are doing is adjusting the ratio of your two responses to life: reflexive and intentional. You will regularly learn from experience instead of just reflexively experiencing whatever happens next.

Your mind will change. Change your mind and you change yourself. Do that and you change the world.

"If people knew how hard
I have had to work to gain my mastery,
it wouldn't seem wonderful at all."

—MICHELANGELO

exercise 1

Where Does It Hurt?

This simple exercise offers a practical, intimate beginning for the process of personal change. At the heart of controlled, intentional personal change lies personal mastery. Think of mastery as an expansion of your ability to produce precisely the results you want in your life. Mastery requires the discipline of noticing what's working and what isn't, what you're ignoring, and where you can grow.

Take ten minutes with your journal and answer the following questions. (Please don't be too analytical. Trust your gut. Write down the first responses that come to you.)

1. Where are you suffering in your life right now? (Or, where are you stuck, where

are you *not* producing the results you would like?)

2. What are the rubs, distresses, upsets, or crises in your life? (Put another way, what mistakes are you in the middle of right now? Is there something unpleasant you are ignoring?)

3. Are there any relationships that are troubling you, or are not as productive or satisfying as they should be?

When your list is complete, make a note in this journal entry titled "Focus." Under this heading select two problems from your list that you'd like to handle soon.

Now make another entry titled "Review." When your twenty-one-day *Profit from Experience* course is completed—that is, on the twenty-second day—return to this entry and file a brief report to yourself on the current status of these problems. As your life changes, this is a good exercise to repeat often.

Awaken
Your Learner

"Unless you try to do something
beyond what you have already mastered,
you will never grow."

—RALPH WALDO EMERSON

T HE MIND HAS TWO PRIMARY MODES of operation. Call them the Auto mind and the Executive mind. Think of your Auto mind as the part of the self that handles your routine affairs. Think of your Executive as the part that pays attention, purposefully changes, and learns new skills when necessary.

Neither mode of operation, in itself, is good or bad. It is good, however—in fact, vital—that you develop the ability to *choose* which mode to operate in at any given time.

Your Mind on Autopilot

LEFT TO ITS OWN DEVICES—when the Executive in you leans back, as it were, feet on the desk, hands behind the head—the mind will spend most of its time running in the Auto mode. There is a certain logic to this: it conserves energy. I call this "low energy matching," which refers to the ability of a system to respond to the demands of its environment with the least effort. Proper use of the Auto mind allows you to accumulate a reserve, to maintain a surplus, of what amounts to high-octane mental rocket fuel for those critical moments in life when the big move, the important decision, the bright idea, or the new direction is needed.

The Auto mind runs the programs for feeling, thinking, memory, sudden reaction. The Executive mind has the capacity to observe this process and to choose which programs to run. Naturally, the division of labor between the two isn't rigid; they often do job sharing. It is the capacity of the Executive mind, however, that must be cultivated.

Executive in Charge

TO ILLUSTRATE: the Auto mind is the only reason a baseball batter can ever connect with a ninety-five-mile-an-hour fast ball. If it were the Executive mind trying to do the job, the batter would still be analyzing the pitcher's windup long after the barely visible ball had already slammed into the catcher's mitt.

But here is an interesting paradox. The Auto mind is also the reason that a pitcher with a ninety-five-mile-an-hour fast ball can fool a batter by throwing a slow change-up. The batter's Auto mind takes in the situation—the count, the inning, the score, whatever body language the pitcher is conveying—and says, "Here comes the heat, get ready, swing," making the batter tie himself into a knot and look like a complete fool as a fat slow pitch floats lazily across the plate. There's nothing like an embarrassment like that to wake up a batter's Executive mind. Now it's the Executive mind glowering back at the pitcher through the batter's eyes, daring the pitcher to throw the same pitch again.

The Auto mind and Executive mind are good teammates, natural teammates, and natural learners.

So while the mind's tendency toward homeostasis, to run in the Auto mode, is usually a good idea, it isn't always a good idea. It's best to keep the Executive in a sort of semi-alert state all the time. You want to let the Executive decide when the Auto mind is equal to the task at hand and when it's time for the Executive to take over.

Alerting the Executive

HERE'S A REAL-LIFE EXAMPLE of the Executive mind at work.

An airline captain in command of an Airbus A300 was departing New York for Mexico City. The plane was gathering speed for takeoff when the pilot noticed his airspeed indicator was stuck at seventy knots.

With the fate of 230 souls in his hands, this is what the captain knew:

- He needed a speed of 160 knots to rotate, pull back on the yoke, and take off.

- The aircraft was performing normally, accelerating normally, and was roughly five seconds away from being airborne. (Actually, he didn't "know" that acceleration was normal. The only way he had of knowing that was his airspeed indicator, and it seemed to be on the fritz.)

Like most senior officers in the cockpit of a commercial airliner, this captain had logged thousands of hours of flying time—over fifteen thousand—in millions of miles of travel.

Knowing about the Auto mind, you know that so much experience creates a lot of tidal pull in the habits of a pilot. Under the sway of such habit, you or I might have said, "What the heck, I know how fast we're going. One, two, three, four, five..." Then we would have pulled back on the yoke. If we had been wrong, the airplane would have stalled, and there would have been big black headlines in the newspaper.

Let the Executive decide when the Auto mind is equal to the task, and when it's time for the Executive to take over.

What the captain did instead was this: he simply said to his copilot, "It's your aircraft." Without skipping a beat, the copilot took the controls, cross-referenced his own airspeed indicator with the airplane's third, backup, instrument, and lifted the plane aloft so prettily that passengers reading their magazines never even lifted their eyes from the page.

Knowing When to Switch

IF THE PRECISE MENTAL BALANCE represented by the consciousness of a good pilot typified all human activity, the world would be a very different place. Thoreau would never have reached that troubling conclusion about most people leading lives of quiet desperation.

Of course, a pilot is trained to switch from Auto to Executive mode at the drop of a hat. But the rest of us can also train ourselves to be more aware and more alive to our own choices.

"We experience what we believe.
If we don't believe
that we experience what we believe,
then we don't, which still means
the first statement is true."

—HARRY PALMER

---

exercise **2**

How's Your Autopilot?

How do you know when the Auto mind process is working for you or against you? There's only one way. From time to time, you must examine your assumptions in critical areas of your life. Once you've brought them to consciousness, you can assess their accuracy and evaluate whether they are a help or a hindrance. Without doing this, the personal initiatives you are taking at any given time are likely to be unbalanced. Your actions will probably be too reflexive and not intentional enough if you do not consciously review them every now and then.

Write down three beliefs you have about each of the two focus problems identified in exercise 1. (Let your thoughts flow freely; don't belabor or edit them.)

Example:

Let's say one of your focus problems is chronic financial stress. Your entries might look like these:

1. I must have some learning disability when it comes to earning and managing money.

2. My parents weren't good money managers. Maybe they taught me their faults. Or maybe my financial incompetence is hereditary.

3. I'm afraid I don't have either the aptitude or skills for earning a secure livelihood.

Now, write down three positive alternative assumptions (you don't have to believe them, just write them).

Example:

1. I can learn to manage money. The truth is, I've never really worked at it.

2. My parents certainly had the intelligence to be better money managers. It obviously wasn't very important to them.

3. I've never honestly worked at developing my skill at doing what I really love. If I did, I know those skills would support me nicely.

In a simple statement, assess the likely consequences of both sets of assumptions.

Example:

I've always had these negative beliefs about myself, and I've never experienced anything but frustration with money. If I started believing in myself, my earning and handling of money would probably improve.

Which consequences would you prefer? Go ahead, write it down.

(Note: This exercise is being used here to inventory assumptions about a specific topic—the focus problems of exercise 1. It can also be an effective tool for shedding light on the general assumptions that so often unconsciously govern our lives. For example, applying it to assumptions about yourself, your health, your job, your family, your relationships, your sex life, your future, etc., can yield valuable clues for personal growth.)

Learning is an increase in personal currency. How will you get it, and where will you spend it?

When You Wish Upon a Star

"We hope vaguely but dread precisely."

—PAUL VALERY

T HE OLD SAYING about being careful what you wish for because it might come true could serve as an homage to the Auto mind. When you tell yourself that you want more money, a higher position, greater recognition, etc., the Auto mind will dependably get to work to set behaviors in motion to bring what you want—or at least what you *say* you want. This is why you might add that you also want peace of mind, a happy family life, good health, etc. Otherwise, the workaholic Auto mind will labor ceaselessly to provide you with the former, perhaps at the expense of the latter.

Setting Priorities

A POIGNANT EXAMPLE is the early retirement of base-ball star Ryne Sandberg. By some measures Sandberg was the best second baseman who ever played the game. But at the relatively tender age of thirty-four, just as the 1994 season was getting underway, Sandberg was on the phone one evening with his eleven-year-old daughter Lindsey.

"Dad, when are you going to retire?" she asked him. "I'm going to be going to college pretty soon."

For seventeen years Sandberg's goal had been to become the best baseball player he could be. With nine Gold Glove awards and ten All-Star selections, more than any second baseman in baseball history, it looked as though he had gotten what he asked for. But his daughter's question made him realize that he didn't have what he really wanted.

It's a good idea to recalibrate dreams and wishes every little while.

Sandberg shocked the sports world when he walked away from $16 million and the two and a half remaining years on his contract to go home to be with his family. One of the things he was most excited about, he tried to explain to disbelieving media, was being able to drive his children to and from school every day.

Ryne Sandburg's decision is surprising to many because it seems anticultural. That is, it goes against society's predominant values.

I share this anecdote in the knowledge that, as a sage once said, life is so *daily*. As far as we know, Ryne Sandburg could decide to return to baseball tomorrow—or reverse Michael Jordan's odyssey and take up basketball (at least for a while).

Life in Flux

THE ONLY THING THAT SHOWS UP CLEARLY in our crystal ball is that life is more like a parade than a statue. Life moves. That's why it's a good idea to recalibrate dreams and wishes every little while.

Like Ryne Sandburg's change of heart, today's exercise might be considered anticultural as well. It asks you to perform a kind of personal inventory that isn't taught in school and is hardly ever reinforced in daily life. When was the last time a colleague, a vendor, a relative, a boss, a customer, an advertiser, or a friend asked you to figure out what you really think, how you really feel, or *what you really want?*

"Reach high, for stars lie hidden in your soul. Dream deep, for every dream precedes the goal."

— PAMELA VAULL STARR

exercise **3**

What Do I Really Want?

We can usually give a quick answer when someone asks us what we want. But the quick answer is rarely good enough when it comes to things that really matter. Often, the desires that lie on the surface of our thoughts don't reflect what we really cherish. This is a peeling-the-onion kind of exercise designed to help you create personal and professional goals that come from the heart.

Page One

On a new page in your journal, write the question, "What do I really want?"

Next to it, write the answers that pop into your mind. When you're done, turn the page.

Page Two

On this empty page, write the question, "What *do* I really want?" Next to it, write what comes to mind. When you're done, turn that page.

Page Three

On this fresh page, write the question, "What do I *really* want?" Write down your answers. Then turn the page.

Page Four

Write the question, "Underneath everything, what do I truly want?" List your answers.

Is there a connection between your insights derived from this exercise and the problems you noted on day 1?

Hurry Up
and Get Sick

"There is more to life than increasing its speed."
—MOHANDAS GANDHI

BY NOW YOU CAN SEE that profiting from your experience requires a steady investment of your time. If you are typical, this is an investment you are reluctant to make. It's understandable if you feel you don't have a lot of time to spare.

If you are willing to live with the above conviction—that you are time poor—then you had better be ready to take the consequences, too.

Hurry Sickness

THERE IS SUCH A CHRONIC SHORTAGE of time these days that doctors have begun thinking of it as an illness, as though shortness of time, like shortness of breath, were a sign of trouble. Doctors call the illness "hurry sickness," says Anne B. Fisher in *Fortune.* Its victims suffer from a sort of delirium; their sense of time is distorted. In busy places, you'll find more hurry sickness than, say, in settings where folks sit out on the porch in the evening and listen to the crickets sing.

Larry Dossey, M.D., author of *Healing Words,* used to practice medicine in Dallas—a bustling place if ever there was one—where he saw his fair share of hurry sickness. One method he used to diagnose the malady was to have patients pull up a chair, just sit quietly for a spell, and announce when they thought a minute had passed. Next door to Dr. Dossey's office was EDS, the headquarters of Ross Perot's company. The worst case of hurry sickness Dr. Dossey ever saw belonged to an EDS manager. "That's a minute," the patient declared after only nine seconds.

The thing is, hurry sickness is not some benign little irritation like hiccups. It is potentially serious. When the mind is forever telling the body to get a move on, speed it up, get the lead out, the mind doesn't just sit back and trust the body to obey. It squirts chemicals to make the body jump when the mind says frog. When you live this way, always scrambling to gain the world for the clearance price of the soul, the chemicals build up and become toxic. Eventually, they will poison the life right out of the cardiovascular system. It is not without reason that the industrious, nose-to-the-grindstone Japanese coined a word meaning death by work: *karoshi.*

The Ecology of the Soul

IT'S FUNNY HOW ALL THIS WORKS, the meteorology of the mind, the ecology of the soul. Milton said the mind is its own place, capable of making a heaven of hell or a hell of heaven. The French like to say that the heart has its reasons of which reason knows not. A 1972 medical study in Massachusetts found

57

that disliking one's job is a burden on the heart more likely to cause heart disease than smoking, high cholesterol, or not getting enough exercise. (Imagine the futility of trying to control health care costs in a nation of job haters.)

The point is, we are exquisitely complex creatures. When we let our programs run us, instead of the other way around, we can lose our way quicker than you can say, "Cogito, ergo sum."

For most of us, learning requires slowing down.

"You don't get to choose how you're going to die, or when. You can only decide how you're going to live. Now."

— JOAN BAEZ

exercise 4

Pace Yourself

When you continually push yourself harder, you grow more and more insensitive to your own needs and the needs of those around you. With your circuits overloaded, you lose touch with your own intuitions and feelings. Under such hurry-anesthetized circumstances, there is no way that you will dependably profit from your experience. You hardly take time to notice your experience.

The response to increased demands on your time does not have to be to go faster. It may be wiser to slow down, drop a few commitments, renegotiate a few agreements, and make some new choices.

Take a few moments with your journal and answer the following:

- Where in your life might you be moving too fast?

- Where do you seem to be losing yourself?

- What situations are piling up on you?

- Should you slow down, take a break, renegotiate?

- Whom do you need to talk to?

- How does the group of people you spend most of your time with affect your pace?

- Who would support you in slowing down a bit?

The Mbuti of Africa believe we are each surrounded by a bubble. It is possible to be moving so fast we outdistance our bubble. They call this state "wuzi-wuzi."

Stay Awake

*"It is what you choose
not to observe in your life
that controls your life."*

—LYNN V. ANDREWS

THE DECISION TO BECOME SELF-OBSERVANT is one of those deceptively simple acts that can change your life. This is because it opens up vast new horizons of choice and possibility.

How do you become self-observant? It's as easy as it is potentially powerful. The most concrete expression of consciousness is being able to state at any moment, to yourself and anyone else who cares to listen, exactly what your experience is. Do that, you're awake. It's that simple.

So let's experiment. Ask yourself right now what you are feeling. What are you thinking? Are you intrigued with this idea? Skeptical of it? Do you find the subject boring? Describe your spirits at this very instant. Are you feeling chipper, anxious, irritated, mellow, tired, energized, curiously sensitive? What? Report!

Those who choose to remain ignorant about what they feel and think, why they do things, why they react in certain ways and hold to certain judgments, are just doing what comes naturally. They are also resigning themselves to the personal equivalent of a flat earth, consenting to be governed by the shadows of the unconscious mind.

The problem is that waking up, becoming conscious, can be scary. Psychologists who have studied this aspect of human behavior say that we tend to sidestep learning who we really are in order to avoid discomfort and guilt.

If much of our behavior is shaped by unconscious choice, and if the headwaters of those choices lie in experiences that shaped us before we had much say in the matter, then maybe we shouldn't be surprised that some of the choices we make, some of the things we do, do not make us proud, perhaps even cause us to wince in guilt. We'd rather not think about it. We'd rather just go on living with that funny engine noise than look under the hood and find out what's causing it.

We'd rather live with that funny engine noise than find out what's causing it.

Facing Our Fears

SO PRONOUNCED IS THIS TENDENCY to edit unpleasantness out of our world that researchers have even documented physical evidence of it. In one experiment, psychologists used special optical equipment to observe subjects who had been instructed to study psychologically troubling visual images. They discovered that the subjects' unconscious eye movements danced around the bad parts, looking away.

Are you willing to stay awake, to be self-observant? Are you willing to face your fears?

My friend John Scherer equates each of our fears to "personal tigers." He tells the story about how, when in the jungles of India, if one comes

63

upon a tiger, the thing *not* to do is run. If you run, the tiger (being programmed to run after, kill, and eat large moving animals) will get you. However, if you stand and face the tiger, it may choose not to come after you.

Most of our fears are real; you fear what you fear for good reason. But if we face our fears, dissect them, make plans to address them, often we will find the courage to stay awake and do what needs to be done.

> *"I have accepted fear as a part of life—*
> *specifically the fear of change. . . . I have*
> *gone ahead despite the pounding in the*
> *heart that says: turn back. . . .*
>
> —ERICA JONG

exercise **5**

Tiger Hunting

Maybe you have a nagging, unexamined fear that you might lose your job—and then what would you do? Or that your spouse might leave you—and what would that mean for you? Or that someone you love might get sick, or even die. Or perhaps a nagging fear of failure haunts you when you take on new projects.

Getting clear about vague worries can free up our mental energies for the real business at hand: what is actually happening right now. This exercise is intended to help you neutralize irrational concerns—we all have them—as much as possible. This will improve the quality of your self-reflection, which in turn will free up creative resources that are now being wasted.

Today, you are going tiger hunting. Your assignment is to name your worst fears. (No real fears you're aware of? Okay, name the things you worry about most often.) Don't forget any important aspect of your life, like career, relationships, health, family, possessions, and so on.

In your journal jot down the worst things that you can imagine ever happening, in each category. Be creative with this. Tell a story of incredible adversity and misery. Be the biblical character Job!

Want to give this exercise a "practical" spin? Identify any worries associated with your two focus problems from exercise 1.

After you've listed your worries, sit back and reflect. Which ones seem most valid? Which are most absurd? For the worries that make sense, imagine three things you could do to address them. Note in today's journal entry a deadline for taking these steps. As you take them, make a journal entry noting what you did and what the outcome was.

Remember, courage is not the *absence* of fear; it is having the heart to do what needs to be done *while* you are afraid.

Pay Attention

*"As my awareness increases,
my control over my own being increases."*

—WILL SCHUTZ

IT HARDLY NEEDS SAYING that the first requirement of purposeful thinking, and learning, is paying attention. But when we pay attention, what is it we pay attention to? This is not a trick question.

When we use our intelligence, it's not like going into the stacks at the library and walking down an endless row of books to pluck just the right volume from the shelf and then turning to the exact page and focusing our eyes on the precise line containing the information we need. Intelligence is multi-dimensional.

Some of our intelligence exists in the form of language; some of it is auditory; some is olfactory. Portions of our intelligence exist only in the form of rudimentary sensations. Occasionally we'll "know" something based on a feeling in the pit of the stomach. Now and again a memory will lie just beyond grasp. It's right on the tip of the tongue. Hearing the name of a place can cause us to remember a song—or maybe just a bit of melody—and that can recall a fragrance. And the memory of a smell can trigger the image of a face, or perhaps just the laughter, of someone we once knew.

A Memory

FOR LARRY RECENTLY it worked like this:

It was twilight and he was camped with his fifteen-year-old daughter on the shore of a mountain lake. There was a small driftwood fire, and the sweetness of the smoke took him back to a specific moment twenty-five years before. Nothing important happened in that moment. He just remembered it. It was dawn and he was sitting in the open door of a helicopter, and a thousand feet below was the Mekong Delta rolling beneath his feet, and the countryside was awash in pink pastel, and the fragrance of cooking fires filled the air like incense.

Sitting beside the mountain lake, he then remembered a kid he used to play football with in high school. Big, easygoing Chet. Didn't like to hit people, afraid of hurting them. Southern drawl. Dad was a minister. Chet with the kindly manner of a gentleman.

Larry picked out his name on the Vietnam Memorial wall in the muggy heat of the nation's capital on a summer night with camera flashes splattering silently like distant lightning on the black marble. There was a faint sound in his ear. It was his daughter's voice. She was saying something about the reflection of the mountain in the lake. But he hadn't really heard because he wasn't paying attention. For just a moment—no more than five seconds—he wasn't there beside a northern lake at all. He was back in Asia.

As a practical matter, all of our intelligence is not available to us at any one moment in time. What is available is only an infinitesimally small part of it, a grain of neural sand that our attention happens to light upon.

What I know "now" is just a grain of neural sand my attention happens to light upon.

Our thoughts come to consciousness one at a time. So our last thought about anything may not be the thought we want to adopt and call our own.

When we take a position, leap to a conclusion, get into an argument, make an important decision based simply on the fragment of neural schemata our attention happens to be resting on at a particular moment—let's not put too fine a point on this—it might be "stupid." Stupid, not in the sense of ignorance, but in the sense of ignoring much of what we know (both cognitively and emotionally). Often, the expression "I should have known better" is literally true.

Stupid Conversations

It's STAGGERING how often most of us make mistakes about which we should have known better. I like to illustrate this tendency in workshops by conducting an informal "stupid conversation inventory." Here's how it works:

With the audience members' eyes closed, I ask for a show of hands to questions like these:

"In the last week, how many people had conversations that needed to go somewhere, but didn't? Conversations, in other words, intended to produce understanding, commitment to action, and so forth, but which were somehow just left dangling? Raise your hands. Okay, good. Now, how many people had conversations, or maybe meetings, that revolved around some point of conflict or difficulty—at work or at home—that never got resolved? The type of conversation we're talking about now is the kind that you play over and over in your mind, maybe recounting it to others, of course emphasizing how bad and wrong the other people in the conversation were. How many people had conversations like that? Hands up. How many people spent more than an hour in such conversations? Two hours? Three? Four? More than six? Okay, good. Finally, how many of you in the last week had conversations in which the parties involved somehow never seemed to come right out and say what they really wanted to? You went away scratching your head, saying, 'What was *that* about? What was he trying to tell me?' How many had one of those little gems? How much time do you estimate you spent having the conversation, thinking about it, and perhaps recounting it to others? An hour? Three? Six? More than ten? Fifteen hours?"

Stupid conversations are triggered when too small a part of our intelligence is engaged.

People then put their hands down and open their eyes. They hear the results of the inventory. In a typical audience, more than half the people report six hours of weekly stupid conversations. A surprising number report fifteen hours of such useless discussions.

Two points. One, stupid conversations are triggered when too small a part of our intelligence is engaged. And two, we never get an audit of what stupid conversations cost us. People who routinely spend fifteen hours a week in stupid conversations at work would scream bloody murder if the actual cost of those conversations were deducted from their pay. And most of us would be horrified if we knew the havoc stupid conversations have wreaked in our personal lives over the years.

Avoiding Stupid Conversations

THE ALTERNATIVE TO STUPID CONVERSATIONS—and this is another key to profiting from experience—is to learn to manage your attention. That is, to manage it routinely, to move it around and take in as much other information as possible in order to bring more of the neural network of life's lessons to bear on any particular issue.

The alternative to stupid conversations is to learn to manage your attention.

Here's an example of how one of my colleagues avoided a stupid conversation. She and two close friends took a weekend retreat at a rustic hot springs resort. My colleague awoke in the night with stomach pains. In the small cabin the friends shared, the others were aware that she never did get back to sleep.

A few days later, one of the women told my colleague that she was very concerned about her health and gave her a stern lecture. Not only was my colleague's health excellent, she was at a loss to understand the high emotion of this dear friend. Afterward, she discovered that she was not only perplexed but hurt and a little angered by what seemed a condescending, parental attitude.

When the friends lunched together the following week, my colleague brought the matter up. Instead of confronting her friend with hurt, angry feelings, however, she simply reported how the scolding made her feel. She asked why her friend had used the tone she had.

"Because I really am worried about you," answered her friend.

"Yes, but why?" said my colleague. "It was only indigestion."

After a few minutes of conversation, the other woman's face clouded, and her eyes got wet. A realization came over her that hadn't even dawned on her the week before. The woman's mother had suffered years of abdominal pain with gall bladder problems, the woman's father had lived out his later years with her and her husband and died of gall bladder complications, and a year or two before, one of the woman's other close friends had required surgery to have gallstones removed after experiencing recurring and excruciating abdominal pain. My colleague's friend instantly recognized that these painful associations were triggered at the hot springs.

Paying attention to this new information made a heartfelt reconciliation automatic.

A good guideline in conversations is to realize that whenever you feel yourself becoming emotional and positioned—when your mind has stopped listening and already started to formulate an answer even though the other person is still talking—that's the time a Klaxon horn should start sounding in the back of your head. It could mean that you are on the verge of a stupid conversation. The solution is to notice what you are paying attention to and ask yourself if there is other information that might be more helpful.

*"What lies behind us
and what lies before us are tiny matters
compared to what lies within us."*

—OLIVER WENDELL HOLMES

exercise **6**

Personal Stupid Conversation Inventory

This exercise will help you begin to notice unsatisfying conversations and take corrective action.

First, after a moment of reflection, list in your journal the stupid conversations you had during the last week. Remember, stupid conversations are those that needed to go somewhere but didn't— they didn't produce understanding or commitment to action, or they left a conflict unresolved, feelings unexpressed, or things just incomplete. You might make a rough estimate of the time involved. Because stupid conversations are costly—potentially harmful to relationships and personal performance—you might also make a rough damage assessment in this regard.

Second, identify the issues you were paying attention to that seemed to be triggers. What other matters might you attend to when similar conversations come up in the future?

Next, return to the two focus problems you selected in exercise 1. Do a quick inventory of any stupid conversations that come to mind regarding them and repeat the cycle above.

(Note: The opposite of a stupid conversation is dialogue. Actual dialogue, which is discussed on day 11, is very different from most semiconscious conversations. The important thing right now is to begin noticing just how much stupid conversation is costing you and to begin neutralizing it by controlling your attention.)

Embrace
Your Mistakes

*"No one who accomplished things could expect
to avoid mistakes. Only those who do nothing
make no mistakes."*

—HARRY S TRUMAN

YOU KNOW ALL THOSE MISTAKES you keep making? Maybe this will help you feel better: you really can't help it.

The very trait that makes it possible for human beings to succeed and prosper, in fact the mental foundation of civilization, is also the characteristic that makes mistakes inevitable. "Success" and "mistake" are simply opposite sides of the same coin.

Welcome to the Human Condition

THE BRAIN IS CAPABLE of such highly focused attention that it can lead to revolutionary ideas and frenzies of new behavior that change the face of society in the space of a single generation. But attention gobbles up energy. So any time the brain can *effectively* get by with low-energy, nonconscious, automatic operation, it's a good idea. Take away our ability to automatically program toward repeating behavior that works—to glide, coast, and conserve at every opportunity—and you remove the very essence of our capacity to create social order.

So why are mistakes inevitable? Because the world keeps changing. And it's a good idea for us not to change when we don't have to. That's how we obtain the most favorable glide ratio, get the biggest bang for our biological buck.

Force of Habit

WE DON'T WANT TO CHANGE. In a way it seems we're not supposed to change, at least not in ways that threaten the sustainability of life, but often we must change—it's a mandate—if we want to survive.

So we have to find our way, weed out the changes that work from the ones that don't. And the way we do this is to make mistakes. The human brain is not omniscient, but it is equipped with phenomenal powers of observation. It can absorb information like a sponge, try to make sense of it, test solutions, disregard ideas and actions that don't work, and go with those that do. This is why it is physically and psychologically impossible for us not to make mistakes. What worked yesterday, sooner or later—maybe next week, next year, in a hundred years—won't work anymore.

But our natural distaste for fixing what ain't broke has a dark side. It leads us to trudge blindly ahead when we should be keeping a sharp lookout for the crossroads. It causes us to go on trying to sell buggy whips long after the advent of the horseless carriage. We continue manufacturing carburetors even when every car on the road is using fuel injectors. What is even worse, we learn to fear mistakes. God help us all who were ever rapped on the knuckles with a ruler for the sin of improperly conjugating a verb, hitting the wrong

It is physically and psychologically impossible for us not to make mistakes.

79

note on a keyboard, or adding a column of numbers incorrectly.

Moral: Get comfortable with the operating system of your brain. Don't kick yourself for making mistakes. But don't be smug either. To err is human, to notice is smart.

Invest Your Attention

WHAT YOU WANT TO DO IS THIS: learn to *invest* your attention. You don't want to go squandering it, because you don't have energy to burn. Nobody does. But you *do* have—we all do, it's the way we're built—enough energy to attend to what needs attending to. So when you see a certain kind of problem, a certain mistake repeating itself, do this: say "Thank you" to the mistake, and then wake up the learner inside you. And now let the learner tell the truth about what is happening. Be honest with yourself. Don't let your past success or habits mislead you with their arrogance, saying, "Hey, this is handled, no need to change! We can just keep doing what we've always done because it's always worked before and, darn, we're good." Adopt a "beginner's" mindset. It's okay to not know, to be wrong occasionally.

> *Don't let your past success or habits mislead you with their arrogance.*

So much suffering in the world is needlessly caused by people who must always be right. This is one reason that excellent companies sometimes fail. They bring together teams of brilliant people who perform together brilliantly; then they erect monuments to their brilliance and begin to grow drowsy together, finally nodding off to the sweet lullabies of old successes. It is the nature of things that the monuments to such companies go on standing, like carcasses empty of spirit, long after the companies have ceased to exist.

Mistakes are just unanticipated and unwanted results. What we need is to become self-observant to the point that we notice our mistakes and then, on the spot, coach ourselves away from them. This is the Bobby Knight school of self-improvement. The Indiana coach will stop a basketball game and coach a player right then and there, not tomorrow during practice. That's what we need to do with ourselves.

> *"When we give ourselves permission to fail, we at the same time give ourselves permission to excel."*
>
> —ELOISE RISTAD

exercise 7

Gather Feedback

While this exercise is designed to help you give this valuable gift to yourself, I know from experience that it can be a little daunting. A senior manager at a major electric utility—a powerful and highly effective woman—told me that it made her so nervous she put the book down for several days. That's taking the exercise too seriously. If you find that it makes you that anxious, begin by interviewing someone who you know loves you—your mother, or your beloved Auntie Jane, who has never once forgotten your birthday. Still too scary? Try warming up by "interviewing" your dog, who probably worships the ground you walk on.

Interview two people today (or tomorrow)—one you work with, one at home. These should be people who are important to you, people who know you well, people you have some history with.

Pretend you are a reporter. You want to hear this person's thoughts about you. The interview can be conducted in person or on the phone. Plan to spend just ten to fifteen minutes per interview, so you can be sure to squeeze it into your day. Take copious notes.

Anticipate that you might feel defensive or angry during the interview. Try just to notice these feelings. You can say to yourself, "Now I'm thinking, 'She's wrong about me,' or 'He misunderstood,' or 'She's got it in for me.' " Just notice the thought and let it go.

Under no circumstances may you interrupt the interview format and give your own opinion or viewpoint. You are an objective reporter.

Begin by telling your colleague/family member/ friend what you are doing. Help this person feel safe in being fully honest with you. Assure her that you will not get upset if she broaches an awkward subject. Explain that you want to find out more about yourself from her perspective.

Take notes in your journal.

Ask questions such as

- What would you call my strengths (at work/in the family/in our relationship)?

- If you really stretched your imagination, what would you say are my weaknesses or areas for improvement?

- If I had any blind spots, what do you think they might be?

- In your opinion, what are the conditions that seem to cause me the most stress or upset?

- Do I get along better with certain people or personality types?

- What kind of activity do I excel in?

- What kind of activity do I shy away from?

- If I were to make one change that would really improve our relationship, what might that be?

- If you had one piece of advice to give me, what would it be?

When you are finished, thank her for her honesty and her time.

In your journal, reflect on how it was for you, your experience of getting this feedback. What do you notice about yourself? Does any of the feedback relate to the issues you identified in exercise 1?

Choose Harmonious Goals

"Happiness is that state of consciousness
which proceeds from the achievement
of one's values."

—AYN RAND

W E USUALLY WISH FOR THE OBVIOUS, what we can touch and feel, the desires that leap to mind, the things that compel and obsess us. Money. A luxurious lifestyle. Prestige. That sort of thing.

Often we don't remember to wish to have the yearnings met that underlie such desires: security, happiness, love, health, fulfillment, peace, evidence that our lives matter, a sense of connection to others. We trust that the former lead to the latter, but our faith is misplaced. This is a very old mistake.

Again, as we notice the mysterious ways in which thought bears fruit, we must take to heart the old admonition about being careful what we wish for, because we just might get it.

There are a few common wishing mistakes. First, too often we don't allow ourselves to wish at all. People often know all the reasons why something they want is impossible. If you have this kind of block, you might want to preface your wish with what you think makes it impossible:

"If I had (a million dollars, a new boss, etc.), I would be able to (write that book, create that new product, etc.)."

Dream Smart

AS YOU START TO JOURNAL YOUR WISHES, just write down all your thoughts, even all the thoughts that you think make your dream impractical.

Another blockage to having dreams come true is not to wish forcefully enough, as though you really mean business. You just drift along, vaguely hoping for things, stewing away in quiet desperation because your hopes aren't met. As you practice imagining a future where your dreams are realized, it might be helpful to use the future perfect tense. "I will have written my play by then." This language suggests to the mind that the act has already occurred, and that there were some specific steps/attitudes/actions that will already have taken place. By such vivid imagining, you will get the mind used to creating images of accomplishment.

Be careful what you wish for; you just might get it.

Visioning is common practice among athletes these days. For instance, you watch the Olympics and you notice the downhill ski racers standing there at the top of the course, eyes closed, swaying to some rhythm you can't hear. What they are doing is making an image, following their mind's eye as it takes them coursing flawlessly through the race they are about to run. This is the kind of image making that sports psychology has brought to athletics. It works so well that it's hard to compete at elite levels anymore without it.

A few years ago a team of exuberant Australian sailors nobody ever heard of did the unthinkable by winning the prestigious America's Cup sailboat race. The Australian skipper, John Bertrand, credited the victory to image making. He believed that Australia suffered from such a national defeatist attitude, such a crushing inferiority complex, that unless his crew could learn to first *feel* like winners—a sensation of which they were culturally deprived—they didn't have a prayer of ever *being* winners. So, against his backers' wishes—they felt he had no business messing with the heads of his sailors—Bertrand hired a sports psychologist.

Frame your wish or your goals in the context of the fullness of life.

The psychologist taught the Aussies to commune with the feeling of winning, long before they won. He went to what seemed absurd lengths to bring the feeling of winning alive. He even had them practice sailing while the recorded sounds of a bow wake were played, a noise usually reserved for the ears of front-runners.

Life Wishes

FINALLY, WE OFTEN WISH for the wrong thing—not just wrong in terms of our deepest longings, but wrong in terms of the outcomes that are actually in harmony with the rest of the world. This may be the worst of what we do, because the true cost of not caring about the welfare of others is separation from yourself.

So remember to frame your wish or your goals in the context of the fullness of life—to include, for instance, enough personal time for your peace of mind, abundant resources, good relationships, sound health, deep fulfillment, contribution to others.

We appear to be bound by some kind of physical law that says we can be truly happy only if we pursue interrelated goals in harmony with the way the world works. Material wants alone are just not big enough to fit with who we really are. This is the mistake that the mythological King Midas made. When asked the meaning of his epic movie *The Ten Commandments*, Cecil B. De Mille said, "People can't break natural law. They can only break themselves against it."

When you start to write and create images about your dreams, you may find some clarity about how they fit with your values, your relationships, your lifestyle.

"Dreams come true; without that possibility, nature would not incite us to have them."

—JOHN UPDIKE

exercise **8**

Close Your Eyes and Make a Wish

This exercise builds on the work of day 3 by giving your mind a chance to practice making images. It also increases the creative tension for change referred to in the rubber-band exercise. Note that you will hang onto some images and throw out others. In the process, you'll have a new neural net to start collecting the thoughts and feelings that will serve your best interests.

List a couple of your favorite or most valued dreams. (Again, you may wish to borrow from the results of day 3.) Choose one at a time. Answer the following:

What does it look like? What do you look like? Visualize yourself performing perfectly. Make your images as realistic as possible; the more vivid they are, the more powerful they will be in shaping your real behavior.

Pretend you have already accomplished your dream. How do you feel? What have you done already to make it happen?

If you think your dream is impossible, pretend that it's not. Say something like, "If only _____, then I could really _____." Write down whatever comes to mind as you are imagining.

If your dream came true, would it be good for others? How so? (If not, how might you modify your wish so that the highest good might be served?)

Return to your two focus problems from exercise 1 (if you haven't included them yet). Imagine those problems were resolved. Repeat the above cycle and make notes in your journal. Remember to visualize frequently the results you want to strengthen the new neural net.

day 9

No BS

*"Nothing is at last sacred
but the integrity of our own mind."*

—RALPH WALDO EMERSON

I KNOW A MAN who speaks a dead language. It's called BS. It's not that he digresses, or is vague, or glib, or displays any other mild, discreet characteristics of less-than-candid speech you might care to use in polite company.

It's just that at work, BS is this man's only form of expression. I don't know if it's his mother tongue, but it seems to be the one language now at his command. Every time he opens his mouth, that's all that comes out. Everyone around him knows it. It may even cost him his job. It's very sad. The man's colleagues and superiors would like to help, but they have nice manners and just don't know how to bring it up. So I bring it up here in the sincere hope that a dissembler somewhere may be helped.

In fairness to my friend, you need to know that his unfortunate speech impediment, in all likelihood, is not entirely his fault. He is to some extent a product of his environment, and until now the environment mandated that those wishing to keep their jobs become expert in the dishonest use of language.

Straight Talk

IN THE OLD DAYS—which ended only recently in my friend's company—all the emphasis was on making numbers. Make your numbers or get your walking papers. That was the deal. But there was only so much the average individual could do to make the numbers, because, as we are increasingly aware, making numbers reflects more on the overall health of an organization than the fitness of lone players within it. Unfortunately, this was a nuance of organizational life lost on many of the old managers.

"I have seen several skilled cons in my practice," noted Anne Wilson Schaef.

> Most were charming, lovable people who seemed sincere and appeared to be generous and giving; all were liars. They all practiced "impression management," which is telling me what they think I want to hear. Usually they were so out of touch with themselves that they did not realize how dishonest they were being. Lying was the only way they knew to try to control a frightening, overwhelming universe.

So people like my friend learned that if the system itself prevented them from playing a good game, they could at least learn to talk a good game. Out of pure survival instinct, they acquired the habit of telling the boss what the boss wanted to hear.

But then things changed inside my friend's company. A new management regime arrived, and the new regime does not emphasize numbers. It stresses values, reasoning that good values lead to the right behaviors, and that adds up to good numbers. And the new regime wants straight talk. My friend is one of the few holdovers from the old days, and he hasn't noticed the change.

This is what happens: one of the new bosses will be discussing some important change, and while the words still hang in the air, my friend is off and running at the mouth. He's saying, in effect, "Yessir, you got it, I'm with you all the way—buddy!" I've been present at meetings when he has done this, and it is embarrassing. His new colleagues look at him like he's a Martian.

My friend doesn't realize how much trouble he is in. He's going to get fired if he doesn't shape up. The new regime is not unkind—quite the opposite, really—but if my friend doesn't wake up soon, he will be regretfully and respectfully fired. His new colleagues have no compunction—none, zero—about putting the needs of the many over those of the few. They realize that BS compromises the common good.

What is wrong with BS is that it dulls the senses of those who use it. It prevents them from noticing change in the environment.

The Real World

BY NATURE, HUMAN BEINGS have exquisite sensitivity to their surroundings. Ancient Polynesians, for instance, were able to settle the 10-million-square-mile Pacific Basin not just because they learned to follow the stars, but also because of the complex interpersonal skills they developed and the amazing feel they had for the world around them. These navigators, it is said, could be blindfolded and taken on a long sea journey, and tell where they were with uncanny accuracy merely by slipping into the water and feeling its temperature and flow against their skin. NASA wants to study their behavior to learn ways to improve space travel.

I think my friend could learn to speak the new straight talk by asking for feedback from his boss and colleagues, and by becoming acutely conscious of his goals and stopping himself periodically throughout the day to evaluate whether his words and actions are taking him where he wants to go.

My friend should practice something I think of as effortless concentration. This involves bringing his senses—his ability to notice, to just listen and feel—into balance with his cognitive abilities, how he thinks about what he feels. Effortless concentration means that you notice how you feel about the data your senses bring you, and that you do not BS yourself or anyone else about it. How are you going to profit from your experience if you ignore it or lie about it?

By nature, human beings have exquisite sensitivity to their surroundings.

Powers of Observation

I SUGGESTED TO MY FRIEND that he practice by eating a single raisin—but instead of just chomping and swallowing, reacting to the raisin as he always does, that he first savor it, notice its sweetness, its various flavors, actually notice how the raisin makes him feel. Similarly, I suggested that he notice how the words of his company's new boss make him feel, instead of just snapping off a reflexive boss-response as the old world required.

"What do you mean?" he said.

"Well, what did you hear?" I asked, referring to a meeting he had just come from.

He thought for a while and said, "Well, he wasn't beating on us and telling us we had to bring in the numbers or you know what. He was talking about the values that need to guide our behavior."

"How did that make you feel?"

"Sounds good," he said. "Makes me feel good. (Blah, blah, blah.)" All BS.

"Come on," I said. "How do you feel?"

There was another pause. His face took on a worried expression, the way a blindfolded Polynesian navigator might look after brushing against an iceberg. Then he said, "Nervous. It makes me a little nervous."

It is one of the first sentences of the new language I have heard him utter. For my money, it's a good sign.

"You never find yourself until you face the truth."

—PEARL BAILEY

Tell the Truth

The world is full of punishment for telling the truth, punishment that often began in the home where you grew up. In many ways society teaches us not to tell the truth. The black art of BS is a skill we all possess to one degree or another.

Telling the truth is easy to extol in the abstract but hard to practice in real life. There seem to be grave risks, both at work and at home, to being fully honest.

But entering the narrow gate of truth leads to the richest experience.

In your journal, answer these questions:

- Are there any areas in your own life where you hesitate to tell the truth? List them.

- Why? (What are you afraid of? What would happen if you told the truth?)

- Think of a recent situation in which you would have liked to be more fully truthful. Bring it fully to mind.

- If you imagined a wonderful outcome, what might you say? What is *your* "truth," your thoughts, assumptions, feelings, and desires?

●   Imagine what the other person would say.

If you are hesitating to share some thoughts or information, simply notice your own hesitation.

You will change gradually. Start by simply noticing what's true for you. Then speak it whenever you can.

Tell Yourself a Story

> *"'Tut, tut, child,' said the Duchess.*
> *'Everything's got a moral,*
> *if only I could find it.'"*
>
> —LEWIS CARROLL
> *ALICE'S ADVENTURES IN WONDERLAND*

TODAY, NEARLY THE HALFWAY MARK of your twenty-one-day *Profit from Experience* course, you begin a new chapter in your journal. Until now, you've been using your journal for exercises only. Today, you will begin journaling in a different way.

Journaling is the practice of keeping a running account of the greatest epic adventure you'll ever run into: your own life.

Journaling is easy. All you do is, every day, sit down and tell yourself a little piece of the story of your life, a piece that happened, say, in the preceding twenty-four hours, and what you think about it, and how you feel about it. You can do it in the evening, the last thing before you read yourself to sleep, or in the morning, the first thing before you begin yet another episode in the saga that is you. Or you can do it any other time you darn well please.

Whenever you do it, a simple narrative line is all you need. Forget style. Two thousand years ago one of the most eloquent writers who ever lived, Lao Tsu, wrote in the *Tao Te Ching*, "True words are not beautiful. Beautiful words are not true." This ain't art we're talking about here. It's just

Lao Tsu wrote, "True words are not beautiful. Beautiful words are not true."

the truth—the whole truth and nothing but the truth, so help you God. And don't worry about being embarrassed. This is just between you and the Creator, whom you can't embarrass (thank God).

What's on Your Mind?

THERE REALLY AREN'T ANY RULES to journaling, except that you write down whatever's on your mind at the moment. The funny thing is, of course, that as soon as most of us, or at least very many of us, grasp a writing instrument for any purpose other than composing a grocery list—and this includes your humble correspondent—our minds go blank. Well, this is excellent! We're the ones— aren't you glad to know this?—who can benefit the most from journaling.

Let's take a hypothetical journal entry:

Woke up this morning at 5:15. It's now 5:30 and I'm sitting on the patio. Really don't have anything to say. Mind's a blank. Looks like it's going to be another beautiful summer day. Not a cloud in the sky, just like the last several days. Birds are starting to fly, and I just saw a pair of hummingbirds. Had a bit of a relapse yesterday, after feeling so good the day before. My energy was down again, and that tickle in my throat was back. It's there right now too. Sure hope I don't get a summer cold again this year like I did last year. At this moment I'm not feeling all that hot, but I think it has more to do with that argument I got into with Al yesterday than my sore throat...

You see? Anyone can do this. What has happened in the entry above is that our writer has simply begun with the most pedestrian statement of facts and then slipped into a little disclosure about physical feelings, which, as it turns out, aren't that easy to separate from emotional feelings. This writer, if he or she wishes, is now off to the races. Where is the cold coming from? Is it allergies, or is there something stressful about this time of year? What's causing the stress? What was the argument about? Any similarity between this conflict and other conflicts? There's no limit to what can be written about. You simply write down whatever comes to mind.

Mind in Focus

JOURNALING MAKES THE MIND COME TO, focus, organize itself, elevate amorphous information to the useful form of written expression. What is cumbersome about this process, and what makes it so potentially transformational, is that thoughts flicker like summer lightning, while emotions flow like molasses in winter. There is a physiological basis for this simile. Thoughts travel electrically, emotions chemically.

The modern world, which worships speed, lures us into an unbalanced life of the mind, separating us from our feelings, estranging us from the affairs of the heart. When we struggle to express thoughts and feelings in words, we engage in an act of powerful integrity. The words don't have to be perfect. Their truth lies somewhere deep inside us, not on the page.

Journaling is a uniquely private way for us to tell ourselves the truth about what's going on in our lives. And the truth sets us free, keeps us from camouflaging the problems in our lives and bumping into them over and over again. This benefit alone makes journaling well worth whatever time we invest in it.

Journaling is also a good way to slow down your world, giving you a better chance of understanding it. We make time by taking time. Journaling focuses a slow-speed camera on blurring events, lets you stop and pay attention and get your Executive mind involved. It can actually help you see what was invisible. It is interesting how often journaling reveals that things aren't what they seem to be.

In order to journal, all you need is a notebook (for now, the same one you've been using should be fine), something to write with, and the commitment to take a little time for yourself each day. Julia Cameron, author of *The Artist's Way*, recommends that you journal upon rising each morning until you fill up three pages in longhand. Other authorities, like the National Training Laboratories, suggest that you focus on three elements in your daily life: events, your reaction to them, what you learned.

Journaling is a uniquely private way for us to tell ourselves the truth about what's going on in our lives.

"Inside myself is a place where I live all alone and that's where you renew your springs that never dry up."

—PEARL BUCK

exercise **10**

Focused Reflection

We learn by doing and then thinking about what we did. Journaling helps us think. I personally don't believe in being dogmatic about how to journal. The important thing is that your journaling be a freewheeling, stream-of-consciousness affair. You don't need that sour old English teacher in your head looking over your shoulder and carping on your grammar or spelling or organization. In fact, the kind of self-conscious holding back that results from such criticism is contrary to the spirit and purpose of journaling. I like Nike's advice: Just do it!

If you'd like a little structure, try this: Think about a recent event or circumstance. Answer the following questions, spending at least three or four minutes with each.

- What did I do that worked?

- What did I do that didn't work?

- What do I feel?

- What were my assumptions or beliefs at that time?

- What was motivating me?

For example, suppose you had a conversation today or yesterday that was incomplete or upsetting in some way, and you're still thinking about it. Answer the above questions about that conversation. Also answer:

- What else could I have done?

- What are some alternative attitudes or behaviors I could adopt?

- What will I do next time? . . .

You may need some help differentiating between thoughts and feelings. "I think she was really wrong" is a thought. "I feel she was really wrong" is also a thought, not a feeling. "I felt really embarrassed when he said that" is a feeling.

This practice of reflective journaling may be the most important exercise of all of these. Six months from now, if you've incorporated only one new practice from reading this book, I hope that one thing is keeping a journal.

If you've never journaled before, it may seem a little weird at first. Keep at it. After you've done it for a while, you'll find it's like an old friend.

> **JOURNAL**
> **Day 10**
>
> *Q. What will I do next time?*
>
> *A. I will try harder to make it clear that professional advice does not imply personal criticism . . .*

Dialogue

"Man's mind, once stretched by a new idea,
never regains its original dimensions."

—OLIVER WENDELL HOLMES

A GOOD CONVERSATION can make you smarter. This is good news, given how much of our lives is taken up by conversation. Effective dialogue lets you discover more of your own intelligence—bringing it to the surface via the mining operation of thought and expression—and more of the intelligence of others.

The bad news is, a lot of conversation—way too much—is wasted. Too often, conversation is more like two related monologues than true dialogue. (The Greek parents of the word are *dia*, which means from one to another, and *legesthae*, meaning to tell or talk.) In the garden-variety conversation most of us are familiar with, what usually happens is that people say what pops into their heads, then rehearse what they are going to say next while the other person is speaking. Little or no discovery or blending comes from such interactions, and only weak commitments to act can result from them.

On the other hand, when people actually engage in dialogue, when they honestly share what is on their minds and in their hearts, when they listen with full attention—not just to hear words but to understand what's behind the words—they bring new awareness, new consciousness, new order into their lives. Clear and powerful agreements can result from discussions like these. Dialogue is an art form, and there is no ceiling on the heights to which it can be lifted.

Words as Weapons

SOMETHING ELSE also frequently happens in conversation: it becomes needlessly hurtful. Not long ago I was a bystander to such an exchange, one which, unfortunately, probably comes closer to being the rule than the exception in daily business conversation.

Dialogue is an art form with no ceiling on the heights to which it can be lifted.

It was over dinner. As is often the case, important business was being discussed. Then it happened. One of the parties to the discussion figuratively slipped a knife into the back of the other person. She asked a question—"Well, have *you* ever worked retail?"—the way a good trial attorney would have asked it, knowing full well what the answer was in advance. In other words, it wasn't an honest question. It was a trap, a dig. A few minutes later, she did it again.

For all practical purposes, not only did the value of that conversation come to an invisible, screeching halt, it became downright destructive. The air thickened with hurt feelings. Verbal swords were drawn, and the rest of the meal was taken up with thrusts and parries. If words had actual physical impact, there would have been spilled water and steak sauce all over the tablecloth. No way could the proceedings have been good for the company, or, more important, added any value to the company's customers. I was there in a professional capacity, meter running, so my feelings weren't hurt, my digestion wasn't impaired. But I'm sure the same couldn't be said for the combatants or the eight other managers at the table who were uncomfortable spectators.

Fortunately, some good came of it—at least I hope so—because as I was leaving the restaurant, the duelists looked at me and said, "We've got to talk." We stood in the parking lot for forty minutes and debriefed the conflict. Genuine understanding and reconciliation appeared to result.

What surfaced in our parking-lot summit was that the manager who asked the non-question question—call her Sue—sometimes feels frustrated with her colleague—call him Bob—because she feels he has a tendency to take a position without either the experience or facts to back it up. For his part, Bob regards Sue as combative and feels that she has a tendency to use put-downs to make her points. What could have happened during the dinner meeting was that Bob could have called a halt to the discussion when he felt insulted by Sue. For her part, Sue could have shared her frustration. It would have taken consciousness and courage for both parties to do this, and some tension at the table would probably have occurred. But the conflict would not have escalated as it did, especially if Bob and Sue were really committed to understanding each other and didn't feel the need to defend themselves from attack.

The real significance is that most conversations carry weight and will have either a positive or negative impact. When you get right down to it, few conversations are actually neutral. Such is the nature of human feelings and the power of words to impact them. When we get irritated or offended during conversation and resort to verbal digs instead of being honest about what's on our minds, a kind of fibrillation of insults is usually the result. When we try to repair hurt feelings by hurting back, these little Hatfield-McCoy feuds can rapidly grow out of all proportion to the merit of whatever is being discussed.

Purpose

THE DIFFERENCE between most conversation and true dialogue is purpose. If your purpose is to help other people get clear about their thoughts and to get more clear about your own, then true dialogue can happen. In effect, you'll be saying to yourself, "I'm helping you get clear about what you think, and you're helping me. I never know what I'm going to say until I say it. This conversation is a discovery process. I can declare what is true for me—what I think and what I feel—and when I truly listen to you I may begin to see things I didn't know I knew."

Listening skill is largely a matter of purpose or intention.

Listening skill is largely a matter of purpose or intention. You learned to listen intently as a child with your mother. As an adult, especially when faced with conflict, you must *intend* to be open to others' points of view if you are to hear their words.

> *"I am not afraid of storms*
> *for I am learning how to sail my ship."*
>
> —LOUISA MAY ALCOTT

exercise **11**

Pick Someone's Brain

This exercise will develop your sensitivity to what dialogue feels like.

Select someone to have a casual conversation with. Draw out his or her opinion on some matter of interest to you. Before you begin, get clear about what you really want to learn from the other person.

Let your intuition guide you in selecting both the individual and the topic. The important thing is to experience in yourself a *genuine* curiosity, even fascination, with the other's views and thread of thought. Don't fake it. Try to actually learn something or gain an insight that might not have occurred to you otherwise.

Write in your journal what you learned about yourself and about your way of communicating with people. Reflect on the relationship between your purpose and your ability to listen deeply.

Who in your life do you need to have a dialogue with, about what? Are you willing to integrate his perspective with yours and discover something new?

Be Quiet

*"Solitude is the furnace
of transformation."*

—HENRI NOUWEN

I F YOU HAVE NOT INTENTIONALLY CULTIVATED SILENCE, you have no way of knowing the gifts it has to offer. Words do not embody what we know, or can know, about the world. They merely approximate it, imitate it. Beyond the reach and noise of words there lives a world that words cannot report. It is a world that can be experienced by the senses, but it is protected from the trespass of words.

To feel the presence of the force of the universe, you have to hush. "Be still and know that I am God" is what Christianity says when it means that in order to communicate with God you must yourself be quiet.

Whatever our faith or world view, most of us intuitively understand the wisdom of this prescription. Moments of silence are the gifts we offer, instinctively, to those whom we most respect. Vows of silence are the highest expression of reverence. In the presence of majesty, we fall silent.

The Value of Silence

THERE IS A SOUND OF SILENCE, and it is unlike any other sound in the world. Silence is not empty, but full of meaning and wisdom that words can only obscure.

There is nothing in the world like a quiet interlude to unplug the Autopilot of the mind, to awaken the imagination, to shake off the fitful unconsciousness that the constant racket of talk brings. Most of us in the modern world are so used to the nonstop bombardment of words that, except when we sleep, we hardly know what it feels like for the shelling to cease. This is an easy problem to fix. Just go for a walk by yourself. With no one to talk to, you naturally will just listen. A quiet neighborhood, a park, a trail in the woods can be nice places to do this, but, amazingly, you can experience profound silence during a solitary walk along a busy street. Unquestionably, the soft light of a forest path or the sweeping views from a mountainside have special powers to restore the soul. But the magic I'm talking about, the real magic, comes from the absence of words.

You don't even have to move to become a connoisseur of silence. Any room where you can take the phone off the hook and persuade people to leave you alone for ten minutes will do. Silence can be experienced in an infinite number of ways, but over the next few days I'll share some of my favorites.

Silence is not empty, but full of meaning and wisdom that words can only obscure.

"Nowhere can a man find a quieter or more untroubled retreat than in his own soul."

—MARCUS AURELIUS

exercise **12**

Time Out

Today's exercise is very simple: just give yourself a break. Sit quietly (or walk alone) and simply listen to your thoughts, interact with them, notice the feelings they bring.

Do this after a meeting where something important was said, or at which something stressful occurred. You don't necessarily have to come to any conclusions—just be here now with your thoughts and emotions. This will help you become clear about what you want to do; it will help prevent knee-jerk reactions, and it might keep you from snapping someone's head off.

Willfully inserting little periods of silence between the important moments of your life will help keep you from operating on Autopilot when you shouldn't. Brief intermissions of silence will engage your Executive mind, revealing alternatives that you might otherwise have missed.

At the end of the day, describe in your journal what this was like for you. Just notice.

Grandmother's Recipe

*"I don't pray to change God.
I pray to change me."*

— C. S. Lewis

MY GRANDMOTHER had an amazing way of calming her spirit. That is, her results, her serenity, were amazing; the way she did it was pretty common. She was a Catholic, and she said her novenas. And she prayed the rosary.

This was a woman who lived what most people would call a hard life. Dirt poor nearly always, enduring floods, wars, husbands dying, brothers dying, children dying, crippling diseases. But she gave off love, and she moved through her life with a floating grace. Like anyone else, she would get crazy now and again, upset by events. But it was never more than a momentary disorientation, like a spell of lightheadedness. The keel of that woman had enough ballast to keep her upright and sailing through all the storms life sent her way. Her ballast was the discipline of prayer.

To create the world we want, we must first create an image of it. And prayer is a powerful form of image making.

If you don't like the word "prayer," you can certainly substitute words such as "meditation" or "deep reflection." By prayer I do not necessarily mean petitioning the god of any particular religion. I mean, instead, communing with an inner source. When you pray, the foundation of the act is not a request made of a deity, but rather an acknowledgment made to yourself. You acknowledge your belief that the divine, a force beyond you, exists.

The Power of Knowing

DR. RACHEL NAOMI REMEN, a professor at the University of California's San Francisco School of Medicine and a physician who works with chronically ill people, discovered her own definition of prayer. "I realized . . . that perhaps this was what prayer was—that knowing," she wrote in the *Noetic Sciences Review*.

> This is quite personal and not easy to talk about. But I realize that, for me, prayer is this knowing. It is an experience of a relationship that never changes, like gravity. Gravity is the way I experience my relationship to the Earth. Gravity is a factor in my every movement. Everything I do takes gravity into consideration, all the time. Even though I'm unaware of it, every movement I make is a dance with gravity. God is like that, a constant relationship, and, like gravity, if it stopped I would know it instantly. But it never does.

The image of the infinite and your relationship to it gives you a sense of belonging to eternity. This perspective can be very illuminating.

In the case of my grandmother, it isn't necessary to imagine what her image of her connection to God gave to her. The results were plain to see. With her sixth-grade education, Grandmother wasn't what you would call an abstract person; she was down-to-earth. When she prayed, it was for what she considered to be the most valuable possessions in the world: peace, courage, humility. The very act of making these requests caused her to see herself as a peaceful, courageous, humble person, and that's how everyone else knew her, too. She was an anchored, present woman. There was a remarkable, clear depth about her. Even in old age, grace under pressure was her hallmark.

Inner Changes

BECAUSE THE EXTERNAL RESULTS of image making can be so dramatic, it is tempting to conclude that that is the real power of images—the way they can spawn athletic victory, recast individual lives, even alter the course of history. But the greatest power of image making is that it changes our inner world. That, in turn, changes our experience of the outer world. This is the absolute that governs all other experience.

If you make the image of yourself peaceful, courageous, humble (or resourceful, lucky, creative, whatever), then these are the qualities you invite to whatever the events of your life are. The qualities do not come from the events. They come from your imagery, and your imagery determines how you deal with the events.

> *"After all it is those who have a deep and real inner life who are best able to deal with the 'irritating details of the outer life.'"*
>
> —EVELYN UNDERHILL

---

exercise **13**

Prayer

Can you imagine having prayer as a small part of your daily routine? Prayer is a powerful variation on the type of quiet reflection we've done so far. Suppose something has happened that is upsetting to you or that makes you angry. Forget about telling yourself not to be angry. That will just remind you of the conflict and make you angrier. Instead, try saying this prayer:

May I be filled with loving-kindness.

May I be peaceful and at ease.

May I see clearly that which makes me happy.

May I be thankful for all I have.

Ten times a day, stop and say the prayer two times. Total invested time: maybe five minutes. Or, if you prefer, do this: sit comfortably, breathe deeply, and repeat the prayer over and over, twenty times. Then be silent. Take a total of about five minutes.

If something is bothering you, your mind doesn't know how not to be bothered by whatever it is. The prayer works, not because it asks the mind to stop doing what it is doing, but because it asks the mind to do something else that happens to be the exact opposite of upset. Prayer helps you remember universal principles that you are committed to.

Prayer like this can help you be more vulnerable in an ironically strengthening way, connect you more deeply with people, make you almost a magnetic personality. This is the opposite of controlling a situation with your intellect. It gets you connected to a deeper part of yourself.

Instead of using this prayer, of course, you can also make up your own. Four short lines seem to work well—they should call forth the state of mind you wish to have. Repeat it to yourself throughout the day. (*I write mine on sticky notes and put them in my calendar where I'll see them often during the day.*)

Experience
Your Mind Anew

*"The pictures you create in your head
often turn into the reality
you hold in your hand."*

—ALLAN HANSON

THE WAY A RAGING FOREST FIRE can generate its own weather, intensely felt imagery can become a creative act of irresistible force. There is simply too much empirical evidence to argue against it.

In one study, people were recruited to participate in a basketball shooting exercise. They were tested to establish common baseline shooting skills, then divided into three groups. The first group were told to practice every day to improve their shooting skills. The second group were told not to practice but to visualize sinking their shots effortlessly, over and over again. The third group did nothing. After a certain period the three groups were retested. The do-nothings scored worst. The practicers improved only slightly. The image makers experienced the greatest improvement.

Average people were taught to envision themselves walking barefoot over a path of burning coals. The evening of the event came, and they sat around a huge bonfire as it burned down to radiant, blistering coals. The coals were raked into the shape of a red-hot sidewalk, and one by one participants removed their shoes, rolled up their pant legs, and took a stroll that convinced them there was more to this old world than they ever dreamed. Though a few got burned, some even badly, most mastered the imagery that allowed them to make the passage unscathed. "It's hot, but not uncomfortable," says John Scherer, a man I know who has walked on fire. "I can't explain it, but I think something happens between you and the coals. The coals don't change, your feet don't change, but something changes between them." Scherer notes that once you complete the walk you have to wipe the hot coals from your feet right away, because they'll burn the moment you let go of the image that they won't.

When we make images, we teach ourselves from experience in advance.

Cancer researchers like Dr. Carl Simonton have concluded from work with countless patients that

> Imagery, broadly defined as the way we think about things, can have a powerful effect on the body. Healthy images lead to healthy emotional responses, which stimulate the body to produce chemicals important to the healing process. . . . Conversely, unhealthy images and emotions can stimulate the production of stress hormones and other chemicals that divert the body's resources away from healing and make it more vulnerable to illness.

I could go on and on, because by now there is an infinite body of literature suggesting that when we make images we teach ourselves from experience in advance of experience. This works, because the mind doesn't treat imagined data any differently than "real" data. Nightmares prove this. You awaken in the middle of the night in a puddle of sweat, heart pounding, muscles trembling, scared to death, all because of some terror brought to you by that master cinematographer, the mind.

The Dark Side

THIS IS THE OTHER SIDE of image making, the dark side, one with which we are all too familiar. Unfortunately, it isn't confined to nightmares alone. It is one of the more curious aspects of human nature that we bask in misery. We slow down to gape at automobile accidents, love a good fight at a hockey game, delight in the sensationalized misfortunes of the rich and famous.

It is one of the more curious aspects of human nature that we bask in misery.

"A constant gripe about the press is that we have nothing good to say about anyone or anything," *Newsweek* columnist Robert J. Samuelson has written. "We revel in sleaze and scandal. We glory in human frailty. We specialize in character assassination. We enjoy natural disasters. Is it true? Of course. The news about the press is like everything else. It's bad and getting worse: our news standards, always low, are sinking lower."

As an antidote to the daily pollution of bad news, Samuelson wrote a column with ten items of good news gleaned from the most up-to-date edition of the U.S. Census Bureau's *Statistical Abstract of the United States:*

1. The productivity of U.S. industry was up ninety-five percent since 1970.

2. The U.S. remained world leader in Nobel Prizes.

3. Car accidents, on-the-job deaths, and heart disease mortality had respectively fallen by a third, a fourth, and nearly half since 1970.

4. Smoking and casual drug abuse were declining, nutrition improving.

5. Between 1987 and 1992, consumer complaints about airline service fell precipitously.

6. Most children still lived with both natural parents; the number of divorces had dropped since 1981.

7. Since 1970, lead emissions to the air were off ninety-seven percent, soot and smoke were down sixty-one percent, hydrocarbon pollution had slumped thirty-eight percent. Houses built in the 1980s used thirty percent less energy than houses built in the '50s. The cars of 1991 averaged 21.7 miles per gallon, compared with 13.5 mpg in 1970.

8. Between 1985 and 1991, foreign tourism in the U.S. more than doubled.

9. About one-fifth of all U.S. adults were doing volunteer work.

10. The nation's houses were getting bigger and better. The typical new home in 1992 had 1,920 square feet, compared with 1,385 in 1970.

Against the daily dose of mayhem served up by the media, cheerful facts like these almost seem to shock the nervous system. Actually, that may be literally true. Barry Neil Kaufman, an author, counselor, and head of the Option Institute and Fellowship of Sheffield, Massachusetts, teaches clients that thoughts are physiological events, complicated occurrences that form in the brain via the elixir of nerves, chemicals, and electrical energy. Seen in this way, says Kaufman, worry is every bit as much an affliction as a viral infection or laceration.

"We want to get people to acknowledge that their discomfort and distress are lethal," he says.

If he's right, then the No. 1 industrial polluter in America may be the media.

In their own way, bad news and worrying are viruses. Maybe yellow journalism, soap operas, and gratuitously violent or sordid movies are deadly pathogens in our midst.

The Power of Dreams

NEVER DOUBT THE POWER of either a dream or a nightmare. That is the point. The humanistic thinker Harry Emerson Fosdick put it this way:

> Hold a picture of yourself long and steadily enough in your mind's eye, and you will be drawn towards it. Picture yourself vividly as defeated, and that alone will make victory impossible; picture yourself as winning, and that will contribute immeasurably to success. Do not picture yourself as anything, and you will drift like a derelict.

Having a different experience of the mind is crucial to dependably profiting from your experience. This is why, down through the ages, meditation has been found to be such a useful tool.

Meditation itself is transformational. It is almost guaranteed to open a new world to you, as countless books and tapes devoted exclusively to the subject can help you discover. I encourage people to explore them.

If you're not accustomed to meditation, the exercises below can serve as a good orientation.

"If one is lucky, a solitary fantasy can totally transform one million realities."

—MAYA ANGELOU

exercise **14**

Meditative Relaxation

Today's exercise asks you to look for the silence underneath your thoughts.

Often, this type of silence is particularly effective in unraveling the knottiest problems. Perhaps this is because what we resist persists. It's funny what can happen when you just let yourself be with a problem quietly—not think about it, but not *not* think about it, either. Just let it go and concentrate on your breathing. What happens is that the little voice that's always talking to you—you know the one, the one that just said, "What little voice?"— that little voice, the little critic who's never pleased with you, the little judge who never let you off the hook once in your entire life, just gets smaller and smaller, and pretty soon you can't hear it at all. And all of a sudden—pop—there's a solution to the problem. And you never even sought it purpose-fully. Sometimes, after a session like this, you can go for hours without judging yourself or others.

Find a quiet place where you won't be disturbed for twenty minutes. Sit comfortably and close your eyes. Then, just notice your breath. Begin by say-ing to yourself, "Breathing in. Breathing out." Adjust your breathing so that it is slow and deep. Inhale through your nose, exhale through your mouth. That's all. After a few minutes you'll be focused on your breathing and you won't need to say anything. Do this for about twenty minutes.

In this type of meditative silence, you simply acknowledge your thoughts. (You really have no choice; the harder you try to ignore them, the more you catalyze them.) In any event, notice your thoughts, and then let them go—like butterflies across a field, like leaves blowing away. One way to let a thought go is just to jot it down. Do this by holding your journal in your lap; scrawl out the thought without even opening your eyes.

When you accommodate your thoughts in this way, you give them a place to live. Thoughts that have been banging around in your mind are now put away. Handling thoughts like this enables a brief systems shutdown, which gives your mind a rest. This gives your subconscious a chance to repattern itself.

Another good relaxation meditation is to find a quiet place, relax, and close your eyes. In your mind, simply start counting backward from twenty-five. Do this slowly, in time with your heartbeat. Every time you get off track, go back to twenty-five. When you reach one, you've completed the meditation.

Forgive

"It is by forgiving that one is forgiven."

—MOTHER THERESA

IN A WORLD WHERE MISTAKES ARE INEVITABLE, forgiveness is a fine invention. It is a simple device with two working ends: giving and receiving. We should all become as handy as possible with both uses of the tool.

People make mistakes. If you're alive, it happens. Along the way, some of the mistakes other people make will affect you. In fact, their mistakes might hurt you emotionally, jeopardize your career opportunities, hurt you financially, or harm your reputation. In these situations it is understandable if you feel upset, angry, or even depressed.

After savoring the full extent of your injuries, what will you do for an encore?

The question is, after savoring the full extent of your injuries, what will you do for an encore? If you want to move on, you will need to forgive the person who has hurt you. Otherwise, you will remain stuck with the upset, unable to extract whatever lesson there is for you.

It is in your mind that the upset lives and breathes, being endlessly replayed in your private and public talk. Those whose mistakes harmed you did whatever they did, and you have the upset.

Forgiving them clears your mind and allows you to be present in the current moment. Forgiveness is one of the nicest gifts we can ever give ourselves. Among other things, it opens up the possibility of creating healthy relationships with the others. With ourselves, too.

A short story: I have a friend who once had an extremely painful conflict with a boss. The boss habitually second-guessed him, jealously undermined his creativity, unconscionably controlled him in a dozen maddening ways. My friend had overwhelming evidence of the boss's guilt, and plenty of witnesses, too. Unfortunately, it was my friend's energy—*vital* energy—that was being sapped by his resentment of the unfair treatment by his boss. Not until he forgave her was he able to fully step into his highest image of himself.

> *"You're gonna make mistakes. You can't worry about them second-guessers."*
>
> —CASEY STENGEL

exercise **15**

Forgiveness List

The following exercise could be used frequently to clear the air, clear your mind, and possibly even repair relationships. In your journal make a list of all the people who have hurt you and what they did. (Go back to childhood if you're still feeling angry toward someone.)

Now, go through each one and say, "I forgive (the person). I release any upset. I am ready to move into a new future."

If you can honestly feel the intention behind these words, a weight will be lifted from your shoulders. If you cannot genuinely let go of the hurt feelings, you might want to jot some thoughts down in your journal, such as, "By staying upset with this person, what do I gain? What's in it for me? Do I need to be right? Do I want peace or upset?"

The beauty of this practice is that once you forgive others (and stop blaming them), you sometimes see your own responsibility in the situation. This knowledge about your own part in the upsetting event or conversation helps you learn and grow. It can lead to changes in your normal interactions with other people.

> **JOURNAL**
> **Day 15**
>
> *Forgiveness List*
> *Who: What they did:*

You may also want to add some action steps to this exercise. Would it be helpful to have a conversation with the other person? And would you be willing to see the goodness in that person as clearly as you see the problem?

You may need to clarify matters and renew the relationship by asking for more information or sharing your own experience.

Ask for Forgiveness

*"Good judgment comes from experience.
And where does experience come from?
Experience comes from bad judgment."*

—MARK TWAIN

T HE FLIP SIDE OF THE COIN of granting forgiveness is, of course, asking for forgiveness.

This is where the brain's imprint from adolescence rears its ugly head: "I know how things are supposed to be," and "I'm the one who's right." Prejudices like these are not the emissaries of reconciliation. We call them by other names—pride, hubris, rigidity—but they result in the same outcomes for everybody. Relationships break down, colleagues won't work together, family members don't speak to each other for years.

If we can remember that this apparently ungracious, less-than-wise part of ourselves is, at least in part, physiologically based, rather than a spiritual deficit, then it can be easier for us to take the incredible, courageous leap—to admit that we ourselves might have actually been wrong about something, made a mistake.

Living with the discomfort of knowing we've caused others to be upset or angry keeps us distracted. All the unspoken apologies and unacknowledged hurt we've even inadvertently caused others become "incompletions" or "bugs" in our relationships. They prevent us from making smart decisions and rob us of our peace of mind.

An important variation on this point involves self-forgiveness. As hard as it can be to forgive others, it can be even harder to forgive ourselves. Say you're prone to workaholism. What that means is that you're going to have to watch yourself every time you are faced with the addictive high of staying at the desk and cranking out one more batch of the fine work for which you are so justly famous, *instead* of getting into the kitchen and cooking dinner for the family. And no matter how hard you watch yourself, you're going to blow it sometimes. So learn to forgive yourself and mean it.

As hard as it can be to forgive others, it can be even harder to forgive ourselves.

"A man should never be ashamed to own he has been wrong, which is but saying, in other words, that he is wiser today than he was yesterday."

—JONATHAN SWIFT

"I Need to Be Forgiven"

Make a list of your mistakes or misjudgments. Then, for each listing, jot down some ideas for what you could do to resolve it. Make choices for your actions. Then move forward and take care of these incompletions.

Asking for forgiveness creates a new orientation that allows you to take a previous hurt or incompletion and reframe it into a positive action.

JOURNAL
Day 16

Forgive Me List

To whom I did it:	*What I did:*	*To resolve it, I could:*

Listen to Your Self-Talk

*"It's what you learn
after you know it all
that counts."*

—JOHN WOODEN

SOMETIMES, WHEN WORKING with my corporate clients, I don't follow my own teachings. Feeling stressed or frustrated, I'll find myself having thoughts like "Those executives will never change. I can't help them," or "It's all over. I've failed," or "I'll never be able to impress that guy. I don't know what I'm doing."

We all know what this kind of thinking does to us. Self-talk shapes our attitudes, our thoughts, and our behavior, and therefore the results we get. It's like a computer program, the mind's software. An incredibly effective phenomenon, self-talk operates in both the conscious and subconscious levels of the mind. The mind will accept whatever you *tell* it. Then, consistently over time, it works hard at bringing the external reality more in line with the internal image.

Self-talk shapes our attitudes, our thoughts, and our behavior, and therefore the results we get.

Obviously, positive self-talk about who you are and what you can accomplish will create the internal framework you need to be happy and successful.

An even more insidious problem—especially when self-confidence isn't a problem—is the subtle deceit and conceit that says, "Oh, I know what's best here." The next time you hear yourself speak those words in the secrecy of your own mind, a good reply is "Maybe I do, and maybe I don't. It won't hurt a thing to get more information from others." Failure to listen is a common cause of shooting oneself in the foot.

The problem is, most of us know this but we still find it hard to change our entrenched negative or reactive habits of thought. The following exercise will help you know your inner voice and take charge of it.

> *"Only the wearer knows*
> *where the shoe pinches."*
>
> —OLD ENGLISH PROVERB

exercise **17**

What Am I Saying?

Keep a pad or your journal handy, and jot down any phrases you say to yourself frequently or when you're under stress. Important: merely list these phrases or thoughts. Don't try to change or do anything with them.

(*You might choose to take a couple of days on this exercise. Take notes at home as well as at work.*)

After you've become aware of your own patterns of self-talk, you're in the fortunate position of being able to change them, to reprogram yourself. You can start to replace shriveling thoughts with encouragement.

Listen for the pessimist in there who says, "I'm a procrastinator." Leap in with another thought: "Hey, I can be decisive!"

If you find yourself saying, "I'm too talkative," follow it with "I can listen."

"I'm a failure" becomes "I made a mistake and I can learn from it."

Be aware that the negative self-talking may be indicative of feelings you have not expressed and need to. Don't deny these buried feelings—name them and then reframe them.

As often as possible, fill your mind with positive, nurturing statements. It may feel stupid or like a lie at first, but over time your mind will accept the new messages. Tell the truth about your mistakes and shortcomings, but don't dwell on them. Nobody is *always* anything.

Speak to yourself as someone who is becoming who you want to be.

day **18**

What Are You Happy About?

"All we are given is possibilities—
to make of ourselves
one thing or another."

—JOSÉ ORTEGA Y GASSET

ONE WAY TO HAVE A BETTER LIFE is to notice what's already working. It is said that what we give our attention to grows.

Therefore, grow what is good in your life by savoring it. Not only will you tend to get more of what you pay attention to, you will also be enjoying yourself more today just noticing what you love and what you already have in abundance.

It may be tempting to think of this exercise as being simply a variation on the old "Look on the bright side" saw. However, I think of it more as a prescription for not regretting one's successes. In other words, it's important to notice if you are being overworked, but not if it causes you to forget that it is the quality and value of your efforts that causes so much work to come to you. It's natural to feel frustrated when a work project causes you to miss a child's ballet performance; you just don't want to stop being grateful for a moment that the child loves to dance, is blessed with the good health and strong body that enables her to move like a feather, and that, incidentally, you can afford to pay for her ballet lessons.

In order to savor the good fortunes of your life, you don't have to numb yourself to what you would like to change. They are two very different things. Address them as such, and the likelihood of achieving personal mastery—of producing the results you want—will increase considerably.

> *"When one door of happiness closes another opens; but often we look so long at the closed door that we do not see the one which has been opened for us."*
>
> —HELEN KELLER

exercise **18**

Count Your Blessings

In your journal write down all the things you're grateful for. You'll probably include things like health, relationships, possessions, physical comforts, opportunities for meaningful work, recreation, friendships, and so on. Be specific.

Take as long as you want. Put numbers beside your blessings. Can you count ten? Twenty? Fifty?

JOURNAL
Day 18

Consider these blessings:

1. Health . . .

2. Shelter . . .

3. Friends . . .

4. . . .

What do you think about this list? Look at it frequently. Post it on your bathroom mirror, or put it on your desk. Pay attention to it. Update it every couple of weeks.

Take Risks

"You miss one hundred percent of the shots you never take."

—WAYNE GRETSKY

NEW TECHNOLOGY AND COMPETITION keep changing the rules and the playing field. Job security is gone for many of us. Entire careers are going away. Plenty of people will have five or more careers in their lifetimes.

Change is the constant, and with it come choices that seem risky. The Chinese symbol for "crisis" is a combination of the characters for "danger" and "opportunity."

One arena in which many of us censor ourselves is in our business relationships. Often we don't risk saying what we think, even though our thoughts and opinions could really help the organization. Instead we play politics or BS. In some organizations, not saying what you really think has become part of the culture, and speaking openly and honestly about difficult or sensitive issues is forbidden.

Overheard in one such company (now faced with the need to quickly change their culture): A manager said, "I'm so frustrated with all these changes and demands being placed on me, I'm just about ready to walk into the next meeting and say what I really think!" I would say, "Please do!"

Where are your biggest opportunities for success, for achieving your vision, accomplishing your goals? Most of them are waiting behind some learning that is beyond some risk.

To grow and succeed, we need to look into those things that seem risky and assess the potential for both harmful and favorable results.

Usually some of the past, some of the status quo, is useful and we should hold onto it. Some, though, is no longer useful. You can learn to let go of comfortable but obsolete thinking.

"You gain strength, courage, and confidence by every experience in which you really stop and look fear in the face."

—ELEANOR ROOSEVELT

exercise **19**

Should I Take a Risk?

Think about your job or career situation.

What are you currently trying to avoid doing or handling?

Whom do you try to elude?

What are your insecurities?

What risks are you not taking?

In your journal, make a list. Then, after each entry, note what possible lessons and opportunities you might find if you were to take the plunge.

JOURNAL
Day 19

- *What I'm not doing:*
  Its risks:
  Possible lessons:
  Potential opportunities:
- *Another thing I'm not doing:*
  Its risks:
  Possible lessons:
  Potential opportunities:
- *Yet another thing I'm not doing:*

  . . .

(You can stop here or do a couple more.)

After you've completed the list, consider what risks you might take now. Whom can you talk to about your decisions?

What actions will you take, and when?

Check Out
the "Truth"

*"We don't see things as they are,
we see them as <u>we</u> are."*

—ANAÏS NIN

MOST OF US OPERATE as if, at any point in time, we personally possess knowledge of The Truth. We've collected information, we've had experiences, we finally have come to understand what's really going on.

The problem is, there's no such thing as objective reality. What we call "reality" is really just shared perception. To find out if our perception is shared by others, we need to hear from other people. Until then, all we have is our own, personal truth, which is based on any number of assumptions.

When you have experienced an upset, a breakdown, a poor outcome, or are stressed out—these are all good times to stop and check whether your assumptions, mental models, or beliefs about a situation are shared by other people.

We run into problems if our thought processes are unexamined or based on faulty assumptions.

We undermine our own intentions if we behave as if certain things are true when, in fact, they aren't.

The following "Left-Hand Column" exercise, developed by Dr. Chris Argyris, is one tool you can use to check out the mental programming behind your conversations and actions.

In this exercise, you recount key comments in an uncomfortable, unresolved, or upsetting conversation. On the right-hand side of the paper, you write what you and the other person said. On the left-hand side, you write down what you were thinking but didn't say.

Example: Tom and I are team members on a project that is central to one of our company's strategic initiatives. Tom has just made an important presentation to the executives on our progress and issues to date. I had to miss the presentation, but I

The Exchange

What I'm Thinking	What Is Said
Everyone says the presentation was a bomb.	Me: "Well, Tom, how did the presentation go?"
Does he really not know how bad it was? Or is he unwilling to face up to it?	Tom: "It's hard to tell. You know how strange those guys can be. Besides, we're breaking new ground with this project."
He really is afraid; he probably feels bad about the meeting. He knows he let the team down.	Me: "What do you think we should do now? I mean, we do have some issues that need to be resolved; we do need direction and resources from the executives."
I can't believe he doesn't care that he's really put the team in a bind.	Tom: "I'm not sure. Let's just wait and see what happens."
We've got to figure out a way to get rid of this guy.	Me: "You may be right, but I think we've got to do something. Well, see you later."

have been told by several colleagues that it was not well received. Tom had rambled and was not able to clearly answer their questions.

Analysis: As I review the script, I can now see that I made several key assumptions about Tom—that he is afraid to accept that he blew it; that he feels bad about himself; that he doesn't care that he's caused problems and is lazy.

Now, these assumptions may or may not be true, but they did affect how I handled that conversation, and if left unchecked, will affect what I do next. Believing that he's fearful and feels bad, I skirt the fact that I already heard that the presentation went poorly. I don't want to hurt him any more and further erode his confidence. When I ask about next steps and he offers no suggestions, I take this as evidence that he doesn't care, and that the rest of the team and I will need to figure out some way to get Tom off the team.

All this happened in about 30 seconds!

The point is not to *not* make assumptions. You can't stop the process. All you can do is *notice* when you have made one, then make it explicit—check it out with others, rationally weigh the evidence, and then decide to keep the assumption or toss it out and create a new one.

> ### *"The first problem for all of us, men and women, is not to learn, but to unlearn."*
>
> —GLORIA STEINEM

exercise **20**

The Left-Hand Column

Start by selecting a recent, specific situation in which you interacted with another person (or people) in a way that did not work, that did not produce either learning or results.

Next, script out a key sample of the exchange on the right half of a piece of paper. Three to five lines from each person is usually sufficient if you select the part of the conversation that was the most troubling.

Then, on the left side of the page, write what you were thinking but not saying at each stage of the exchange.

Finally, analyze this information to see what your assumptions were.

You behaved as if they were true; are they really?

You didn't say what you were thinking; you avoided dealing directly with your assumptions about the other person and the situation. What did this avoidance cost you regarding your relationship and a clear course of action? Are you willing to go back and confirm your assumptions with the other person? What will you do now?

Doing this exercise frequently will hone your ability to notice your assumptions while you're creating them. Then you can choose to pull them explicitly into the conversation or not, but at least you'll be clear where you're coming from.

Celebrate
Your Nature

"Experience is not what happens to you;
it is what you do
with what happens to you."

—ALDOUS HUXLEY

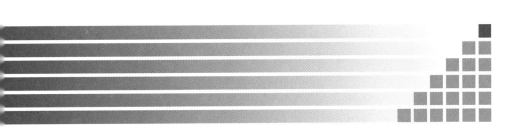

DURING HIS LIFETIME no one knew more about how the mind and body are affected by stress than Dr. Hans Selye. But although Dr. Selye had devoted his life to the study of the subject, you might say that he went to his grave knowing more than he could explain. As an old man, Dr. Selye was diagnosed with a deadly form of cancer. He declined the pain-killing medicine offered him, saying that he had lived long and happily and knew enough about stress to manage pain without drugs. Dr. Selye's cancer, miraculously, disappeared.

Because of his prestige in medical circles, medical authorities asked him how it happened. He tried to explain by suggesting that there is a "biological moral code."

It has three elements, he said:

- Self-knowledge
- A loving spirit
- Respect for nature

People who really know themselves and don't overstress themselves, people who "hoard the goodwill of others" (that's how he put it), and those who respect the primacy of nature, who don't go around trying to fool Mother Nature so they can get away with a destructive lifestyle, tend to be rewarded with vigorous health, said Dr. Selye.

He also said that while certain events in the operation of the brain could be medically explained, certain first events, certain primary instructions given to the brain, could not.

The mind is a piece of work, he seemed to be saying, and it's more than we can understand. You might say it's worthy of some kind of reverence. There are 10 billion neurons in the brain, each of them capable of connecting to thousands of other neurons. It is this staggering network of intelligence that gives us the potential to become infinitely more conscious, to systematically decrease the mistakes we make, extract more and more learning from our experience, and build lives of ever-increasing effectiveness and satisfaction.

We ought to live our lives in cycles of planning, doing, and reflecting.

Cycles of Living

WE OUGHT TO LIVE OUR LIVES in cycles of planning, doing, and reflecting. These aspects of our actions and behaviors can form a continuous circle or spiral. Most of us, though, are great at *doing*, okay with *planning*, and lousy at *reflecting*. So to learn from our experience, we need to spend extra time on the reflection part of the cycle. Most of the exercises in this book have been based on this principle.

As you become more familiar with the process of reflection, you will be able to stop at any time—while you're planning an action, formulating what

163

you will say in a conversation, or taking an action—and reflect.

Perhaps your values complement Dr. Selye's "biological moral code."

However you conceive of your own purpose, you'll find more ways to express it when you take this essential step.

> *"The more you listen to the voice within you, the better you will hear what is sounding outside."*
>
> —DAG HAMMARSKJÖLD

exercise **21**

Pause and Reflect

Plan to take at least twenty minutes of quiet, uninterrupted time. Have a comfortable chair, and put your journal nearby.

Bring to mind the question, issue, problem, concern, or idea that you want to think about now. Perhaps it's one, or both, of your focus problems from exercise 1.

Close your eyes and relax your body. Take several deep breaths, breathing in slowly through your nose, holding your breath for five to ten seconds, and slowly releasing it through your mouth.

Think of the specific issue and just let it float in your mind. (I've found that posing your concern as a question works best.) If other unrelated thoughts or distractions come up, just let them float away.

Keep breathing deeply and slowly.

As you relax more fully and distracting thoughts float away, your unconscious will offer up images, feelings, and ideas related to your questions. Don't try to evaluate them, just jot down key words or phrases and return to your inner space to see what else comes up.

The key is to be gentle and easy with yourself. Allow yourself to be open, to surrender. You'll be letting go of your active, talkative, goal-oriented conscious self in order to find the ideas and connections that exist deep in your memory.

If this is hard for you, do it several times a week for three weeks, and then evaluate your results. It takes a while to program the mind to be quiet on command.

Day 22
and Beyond

"Practice is the best of all instructors."

— PUBLILIUS SYRUS

PRACTICE MAKES PERFECT — when you know what you're doing. Now that you've completed the preceding readings and exercises, you have begun a journey of knowing more precisely how to manage your mind. To master this skill and continue to profit from your experience, you will need to practice for the rest of your life; you will need to remind yourself consistently to do the exercises and to accept the discipline of personal mastery. As you repeat your daily spiral of planning, doing, and reflecting, remember to use actively the four practices I introduced on day 1.

Raising Consciousness

REMEMBER TO WAKE UP FREQUENTLY! Pay attention. Notice what is going on with yourself when things are not working. How do you feel? What do you think? What do you want? Shift from the Auto

Mind to the Executive Mind. Spend the energy and get the insights.

Imagining

USE YOUR ABILITY TO CREATE POWERFUL IMAGES in your mind's eye. See what you really want to see. Imagine *you* behaving how you want to behave; see yourself producing the results you want to produce. When you are facing new challenges, when you are fearful, when you lack energy or feel lost, engage your image-making ability and give yourself something to aim toward.

Framing and Reframing

WHEN DISCORD, UPSET, PROBLEMS, OR FAILURE signal that it's time to learn something, a good place to begin is with your own assumptions and beliefs surrounding the issue. Peel the "layers of the onion" to find how you have framed, and hence perceived, the circumstance. What were implicit assumptions about the other, about yourself, about the outcomes? Notice what your perceptual frame was when you entered the situation; what were you looking to see? Are your beliefs and assumptions working for you or against you? If they are working against you, reframe. Construct a new context in which to act. Remember constantly to build into your life the attitudes and beliefs that will help you achieve your highest commitments.

Integrating Perspectives

ASK AND YOU SHALL RECEIVE. Most people in most circumstances are happy, even thrilled, to be asked their opinions, and often that's precisely what we need to solve our problems and get satisfaction from our daily pursuits. By combining our perspectives, our different points of view, we see a more complete picture. Like the fabled seven blind men each perceiving a different part of the elephant, together we can see what is so.

In your daily practice, notice when your ego has seized control and left you with "rights disease." Take a deep breath and inquire of others' points of view. Listen to them as if they could be right, and allow your mind to entertain several points of view consecutively.

Truth is sometimes an elusive thing, but the truth and understanding we create together may be the truest of all.

"There's only one thing more painful than learning from experience, and that is not learning from experience."

—ARCHIBALD MACLEISH

A Word about Life

"Life is a succession of lessons
which must be lived to be understood."

—RALPH WALDO EMERSON

"AFTER ALL, WHAT'S A LIFE, ANYWAY? We're born, we live a little while, we die."

With those words, a beloved heroine touched the conscience of millions.

In case you haven't read the book to your kids or watched the movie, I'm talking about the central character in E. B. White's classic *Charlotte's Web*. In the scene under discussion, Charlotte is making her deathbed speech to the pig Wilbur, whose life Charlotte and the farm girl Fern succeeded in saving. Poor Wilbur is consumed with grief at the idea of losing a dear friend. Charlotte tries to comfort him:

> A spider's life can't help being something of a mess, with all this trapping and eating flies. By helping you, perhaps I was trying to lift up my life a trifle. Heaven knows anyone's life can stand a little of that.

The spider's observation rings true with most of us—life can't help being something of a mess. And in a way, the real purpose of this book is to help readers lift up their lives a trifle by being a little more conscious in the conduct of them.

I would like to leave you with a suggestion: while our personal growth is probably the most important undertaking that any of us make, and while books like this one can be of assistance, nobody is really qualified to tell anyone else how to live. Be skeptical of anyone who tries. However, I do believe that each of us comes fully equipped with the intuition necessary to

- Make sense of life
- Have a satisfied mind
- Contribute to the world

The point of the exercises you've just completed is to lead you into conversations with yourself—and others, too—to help bring out the deep wisdom within you. Chances are, the conversations won't cause lightning-bolt transformation of your life. More likely, they will help create moments of consciousness along your daily spiral of planning, doing, and reflecting.

The insights and new behaviors that result obviously do not constitute a quick fix. But if you continue to practice simple daily disciplines such as these—especially the habit of keeping a journal—they can't help but maintain a healthy tension on the rubber band of personal change, pulling your life in the direction you want it to go.

"Whatever you can do or think you can, begin it. Boldness has genius, power and magic in it."

—JOHANN WOLFGANG VON GOETHE

Your Personal Journal

_____

_____

_____

_____

_____

_____

_____

_____

_____

_____

_____

_____

"When you choose to write using yourself as the source of the story, you are choosing to confront all the silences in which your story has been protectively wrapped. Your job as a writer is to respectfully, determinedly, free the story from the silences and free yourself from both."

— C H R I S T I N A
B A L D W I N

_____

_____

_____

_____

_____

_____

*"We are not
human beings having
a spiritual experience,
we are spiritual beings
having a human
experience."*

—PIERRE
TEILHARD
DE CHARDIN

"Mistakes are part of the dues one pays for a full life."

—SOPHIA LOREN

"Learning without thought is labor lost; thought without learning is perilous."

— Confucius

"Life is the only game in which the object of the game is to learn the rules."

—ASHLEIGH BRILLIANT

*"Vision without action
is daydreaming, but
action without vision is
just random activity."*
—JOEL BARKER

*"All the world's ills
stem from the fact that
a man cannot sit
in a room alone."*

— BLAISE
PASCAL

"The world we have created today has problems which cannot be solved by thinking the way we thought when we created them."

—ALBERT EINSTEIN

"*Experience is the child of Thought, and Thought is the child of Action. We cannot learn men from books.*"

— BENJAMIN
DISRAELI

*"No journey carries
one far unless, as it
extends into the world
around us, it goes an
equal distance into
the world within."*

—LILLIAN
SMITH

"Experience does not err; only your judgments err by expecting from her what is not in her power."

—LEONARDO DA VINCI

"Talent is nurtured in solitude; character is formed in the stormy billows of the world."

—JOHANN WOLFGANG VON GOETHE

> *"People learn
> from their failures.
> Seldom do they learn
> anything from success."*
> — HAROLD
> GENEEN

*"Courage is the price
that Life exacts
for granting peace."*
—AMELIA
EARHART

> *"There are some things you learn best in calm, and some in storm."*
>
> — WILLA CATHER
> *THE SONG OF THE LARK*

Notes

Page 21–2, 24–5   Dr. Robert B. Livingston. "Why Don't You See Things My Way?" *Timeline*, July/August 1992, 3–5.

28–9   Walter Kiechel III. "A Manager's Career in the New Economy." *Fortune*, April 4, 1994, 68–72.

29   James Kouzes and Barry Posner. *Credibility: How Leaders Gain and Lose It, Why People Demand It.* San Francisco: Jossey-Bass, 1993.

56–8   Anne B. Fisher. "Welcome to the Age of Overwork." *Fortune*, November 30, 1992, 64–71.

93   Anne Wilson Schaef. *When Society Becomes an Addict.* New York: Harper Collins, 1988, 52–53.

103   Julia Cameron. *The Artist's Way: A Spiritual Path to Higher Creativity.* Los Angeles: Tarcher/Perigee, 1992.

121   Dr. Rachel N. Remen. "Pray Without Ceasing." *Noetic Sciences Review*, Summer 1993, 23–26.

127   Dr. Carl Simonton (interviewed)."How to Use Imagery: Inner Wisdom to Conquer Illness." *Bottom Line*, February 15, 1994, 11–12.

128–9   Robert J. Samuelson. "Here's Some Good News, America." *Newsweek*, January 31, 1994, 51.

130   This quote was attributed to Harry Emerson Fosdick in a September 8, 1988 seminar, "How to Tap the Inner Potential of Your Mind." I do not know its origin.

162   Dr. Hans Selye presented these ideas in an oncology seminar at the Sloan-Kettering Institute. His speech was reprinted in *Surgical Practice News*, May 1980.

Reading List

Allen, James. *As a Man Thinketh.* White Plains, New York: Peter Pauper Press, 1948. The classic little book on the impact of thought on health, purpose, achievement, ideals, and serenity.

Cameron, Julia. *The Artist's Way: A Spiritual Path to Higher Creativity.* Los Angeles: Tarcher/Perigee, 1992. An inspired yet practical guide to discovering and recovering one's creative self.

Dossey, Larry. *Healing Words: The Power of Prayer and the Practice of Medicine.* San Francisco: HarperSanFrancisco, 1993. A medical documentation of the connection between spirit and body, this book is a thoughtful, eloquent, compelling treatment on the relationships among prayer, health, and healing.

Gia-fu Feng and Jane English. *Tao Te Ching.* New York: Alfred A. Knopf, 1972. A clear and contemporary translation of the Chinese master Lao Tsu.

Heider, John. *The Tao of Leadership: Leadership Strategies for a New Age.* New York: Bantam Books, 1985. Provides simple and clear advice on how to be a leader by changing oneself, by paying attention to process, and by inspiring others to become their own leaders.

Leonard, George. *Mastery: The Keys to Success and Long-Term Fulfillment.* New York: NAL/Penguin Books, 1991. A powerful little book that draws on Zen philosophy to show how mastery is a journey rather than perfection.

McGartland, Grace. *Thunderbolt Thinking.* Austin, Texas: Bernard-Davis, 1994. A great "how-to" book that will help you transform your insights into business results; includes specific techniques; useful for individuals and teams.

McGee-Cooper, Ann. *You Don't Have to Go Home from Work Exhausted*. New York: Bantam Books, 1992. This personalized guide for energizing your work habits and thinking patterns will help you enjoy work and home life more.

Nhat Hahn, Thich. *The Miracle of Mindfulness: A Manual on Meditation*. Boston: Beacon Press, 1975. A Zen master's method of meditation, concentration, and relaxation; includes instructions for various meditation exercises.

Scherer, John, and Larry Shook. *Work and the Human Spirit*. Spokane, Washington: John Scherer and Associates, 1993. A provocative book that chronicles the personal transformation experiences of a number of successful executives who lost and then rediscovered something vital—their spirit—on the way to the top.

Tart, Charles T. *Living the Mindful Life: A Handbook for Living in the Present Moment*. Boston: Shambhala Publications, 1994. A wonderful integration of ancient wisdom and contemporary science that yields practical exercises for increasing one's mindfulness.

The O'Brien Group

The O'Brien Group works with organizations and executives throughout the world, helping them better adapt to change and manage their own development.

The O'Brien Group is one of the country's premier executive leadership consulting firms. The O'Brien Group helps CEOs, senior executives and executive teams at Fortune 1000 companies work with greater purpose and authenticity. O'Brien Group's team of former corporate executives and psychologists helps their clients hone their leadership skills and improve the performance of their organizations. Current and former clients include Bayer, Convergys, Catholic Healthcare Partners, Sun Life Financial, Express and LensCrafters.

Dr. O'Brien is a popular speaker and has spoken at association and executive meetings throughout the world, from the American Management Association to the American Society for Training and Development.

Contact the O'Brien Group at: www.obriengroup.us

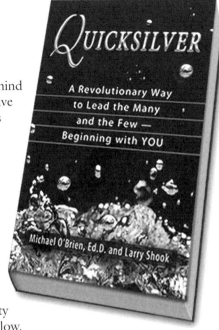